Published by: Matthew Aziz

© **Copyright 2020 - All rights reserved.**

The content contained within this book may not be reproduced, duplicated or transmitted without direct written permission from the author or the publisher.

Under no circumstances will any blame or legal responsibility be held against the publisher, or author, for any damages, reparation, or monetary loss due to the information contained within this book, either directly or indirectly.

Legal Notice:

This book is copyright protected. It is only for personal use. You cannot amend, distribute, sell, use, quote or paraphrase any part, or the content within this book, without the consent of the author or publisher.

Disclaimer Notice:

Please note the information contained within this document is for educational and entertainment purposes only. All effort has been executed to present accurate, up to date, reliable, complete information. No warranties of any kind are declared or implied. Readers acknowledge that the author is not engaging in the rendering of legal, financial, medical or professional advice. The content within this book has been derived from various sources. Please consult a licensed professional before attempting any techniques outlined in this book.

By reading this document, the reader agrees that under no circumstances is the author responsible for any losses, direct or indirect, that are incurred as a result of the use of information contained within this document, including, but not limited to, errors, omissions, or inaccuracies.

Table of Contents

Introduction 2

Chapter 1 - What Is an Option Trading and Types of Option Trading .. 8

Chapter 2 - How Options Trading Works... 45

Chapter 3 - The Basics of Options Trading 56

Chapter 4 - Strike Price.. 61

Chapter 5 - Covered Calls 70

Chapter 6 - Buying Calls 85

Chapter 7 - Volatility in The Markets... 102

Chapter 8 - Buying and Selling Puts of an Option Trading 114

Chapter 9 - Options Trading Jargon 121

Conclusion 160

Introduction

Our introduction to options trading is a comprehensive resource produced specifically for those that are considering trading options but have very little relevant knowledge and experience. If you are completely new to trading options, then we would strongly recommend that you read this introductory section in its entirety before deciding whether it's the right form of investment for you.

Options trading is a relatively complex subject, certainly when compared to some of the forms of investment such as buying stocks, and many people are put off by the very idea of getting involved. There is indeed a lot that beginners need to learn about before actually getting involved and starting to trade options, but the time and effort required can be very rewarding in the long run.

Although it's a complicated subject, it's not that difficult to learn about the important fundamentals. Once you have an understanding of what options contracts are and the basic concepts of what is involved in them, the more complex aspects will make sense to you. Please see below for full details of what our introduction covers.

Options give a trader another dimension to speculate on the market. Used properly, they can be a very beneficial tool. The first thing to know about options is what they are. An option gives the buyer the right to take any action on a particular security at a certain price within a certain time frame. These "rights" are homogenized and trade on exchanges, similar to the way stocks do.

Definitions – Some Basic Terms

The security that the buyer has the right to take action on is called the underlying. If you buy an option, you are long. If you sell an option, you are short. There are two sides to every option, the buyer and the seller. The seller should fulfill the buyer's right. Each side has agreed with the other. Therefore, we refer to an option as an option contract. You can buy and sell multiple contracts at once, the same way you can buy and sell multiple shares of stock. The price that the option contracts are exchanged at is called a premium. The price of the underlying, that the option buyer has the right to buy or sell at is called the strike price. The date that the contract runs out on is called the expiration date. There are two types of options:

A call gives the owner the right to buy a security at a particular price. A put, gives the owner the right to sell a security at a particular price.

You can see the payoff of a long call and put it below. The option value will be negative until the underlying is equal to the strike price. It then moves up in value. A call moves up in value as the underlying moves up in price because you have the right to buy.

A put moves up in value as the underlying moves down in price, because you have the right to sell. Both options loss is limited to the premium paid. They both have an unlimited amount of potential profit.

Definition Of An Options Contract

Options are very different from a lot of other financial instruments such as commodities, stocks, and currencies. Although they are an asset in their own right, they are financial contracts that are based on other financial instruments. They are a form of derivative, meaning that they principally derive their value from another asset.

The asset from which they derive their value is known as the underlying asset or underlying security and options are contracts that allow for the future transaction of an underlying asset between the two parties of the contract. Options contracts contain several terms relating to exactly what that future transaction will be. For example, they will state what the underlying asset is, what the price is, at what point in time it can be transacted, and whether it can be bought or sold.

What Is Options Trading?

There are many different ways to invest and many different financial instruments that can be used for investment and trading purposes. Like all forms of trading, options trading has its unique characteristics and, as we have already mentioned, it's somewhat more complicated than a lot of the alternatives. However, the basic concept is very similar to any other form of investment; the goal is to make profits through the buying and selling of financial instruments.

Although options contracts are one of the more complex financial instruments, ultimately the principle of investing and trading them is of course still to make money. Options trading offers many different ways to make profits from the price movements of a range of assets and securities. Even though they aren't particularly straightforward when compared to simply buying stocks, the potential rewards can make learning how to trade options successfully very worthwhile indeed.

Why Trade Options?

The obvious answer to this question is to make money. For the most part, this answer is entirely accurate. However, given that there are much simpler ways to make money, it's reasonable to ask why anyone would choose to trade options instead of, for example, just buying stocks that are expected to rise in value. There are several good reasons for doing so because options contracts offer several advantages over other financial instruments. Options trading might not be for everyone, of course, but there is plenty about it that investors might find appealing when they discover just what the potential benefits are.

Where To Trade Options

Another important consideration for anyone that is looking to get involved with options trading is exactly how and where they will trade options. Although it's relatively easy to buy and sell options contracts on options exchanges around the world, members of the public cannot make their transactions without the services of a suitable broker. There are many, many different options brokers to choose from and these brokers come in various types. One of the more important decisions you will have to make before you start is which broker you are going to use.

How Options Work: Pricing, Exercising & Settlement

In addition to knowing exactly what an options contract is and what its various characteristics are, it's also necessary to be aware of how they work. We have already explained that they are a little more complex than most other financial instruments and certain features are especially important to understand. In particular, the way they are priced using two components (intrinsic value and extrinsic value), how they can be exercised, and how they are settled are fundamental to options trading. To explain these aspects, we have produced a subsection that specifically covers the three elements of pricing, exercising, and settlement.

Options Trading: Key Terms & Phrases

There are several terms and phrases relating to options trading that are frequently used, and beginners really should ensure that they are familiar with such terms. We have compiled a list of these important terms and phrases and included detailed explanations of what they mean and in what context they are used.

Chapter 1 - What Is an Option Trading and Types of Option Trading

What Is An Option?

An option is a financial instrument giving the right, but not the obligation, to buy or sell an asset, such as a share or currency, for a predetermined price at a fixed future date. An option is a financial contract that gives an investor the right, but not the obligation, to either buy or sell an asset at a pre-determined price (known as the strike price) by a specified date (known as the expiration date).

Options are conditional derivative contracts that allow buyers of the contracts (option holders) to buy or sell a security at a chosen price. Option buyers are charged an amount called a "premium" by the sellers for such a right. Should market prices be unfavorable for option holders, they will let the option expire worthless, thus ensuring the losses are not higher than the premium. In contrast, option sellers (option writers) assume greater risk than the option buyers, which is why they demand this premium.

Options are divided into "call" and "put" options. With a call option, the buyer of the contract purchases the right to buy the underlying asset in the future at a predetermined price, called exercise price or strike price. With a put option, the buyer acquires the right to sell the underlying asset in the future at the predetermined price.

Options Are A Type Of Derivative

Based on the underlying securities, such as stocks, options contracts can be of two major types:

1. Call options allow traders to BUY the underlying asset at a specified price within a specified period or Call options to allow the holder to buy the asset at a stated price within a specific timeframe.

2. Put options allow traders to SELL the underlying asset at a specified price within a specified period or Put options allow the holder to sell the asset at a stated price within a specific timeframe.

Explanation

Call Options: This contract gives you the right to buy an underlying asset at a specific price and date. Call options are profitable if the asset price rises. For example, in the example above where you have a call option for coffee at $1.10 per ounce on Jan. 1, the option will be profitable if coffee costs $1.20 on Jan. 1 because your contract lets you buy coffee for $0.10 less than it's worth on Jan. 1.

Put Options: This contract gives you the right to sell an underlying asset at a specific price and date. Put options profit if the asset's price declines. For example, say you have a put option for coffee at $1.10 on Jan. 1. If the price of coffee declines to $0.90 on Jan. 1, your contract will give you the right to sell it for $0.20 more than it's worth on Jan. 1.

A contract that expires in a profitable position is called "in the money." Unprofitable contracts are "out of the money."

A stock contract, more commonly known as a stock option, gives you the right to buy or sell shares of stock. These are very common as a perk of employment for corporate officers. Companies will often give executives stock options as part of their compensation, in which they have the option to buy the company's stock for a given (typically low) price after several years of employment.

An option is a future opportunity to buy an asset priced today. If the price is lower than it is today, the option can be allowed to expire. That means the investor or trader loses only the original cost of the option. If it is higher, the option-holder makes a profit or Each option contract will have a specific expiration date by which the holder must exercise their option. The stated price on an option is known as the strike price. Options are typically bought and sold through online or retail brokers.

An option contract is a form of financial asset known as a "derivative." Purchasing an option contract it gives you the right to buy or sell some underlying asset on specific terms. You choose a price and date on which to trade this asset. When the time comes, you can choose to execute the contract if it's profitable or let it expire if not. Here's what you need to know about option contracts.

What Does Options Trading Involve?

In very simple terms options trading involves buying and selling options contracts on the public exchanges and, broadly speaking, it's very similar to stock trading. Whereas stock traders aim to make profits through buying stocks and selling them at a higher price, options traders can make profits through buying options contracts and selling them at a higher price. Also, in the same way, that stock traders can take a short position on stock that they believe will go down in value, options traders can do the same with options contracts.

In practice, however, this form of trading is far more versatile than stock trading. For one thing, the fact that options contracts can be based on a wide variety of underlying securities means that there is plenty of scopes when it comes to deciding how and where to invest. Traders can use options to speculate on the price movement of individual stocks, indices, foreign currencies, and commodities among other things and this presents far more opportunities for potential profits.

When trading stocks you have two main ways of making money, through taking either a long position or a short position on a specific stock. If you expected a particular stock to go up in value, then you would take a long position by buying that stock to sell it later at a higher price. If you expected a particular stock to go down in value, then you would take a short position by short selling that stock with the hope of buying it back later at a lower price. In options trading, there's more choice in the way trades can be executed and many more ways to make money.

It should be made clear that options trading is a much more complicated subject than stock trading and the whole concept of what is involved can seem very daunting to beginners. There is certainly a lot you should learn before you get started and invest your money. With that being said, however, most of the fundamentals aren't that difficult to comprehend. Once you have grasped the basics, it becomes much easier to understand exactly what options trading is all about.

Below We Explain In More Detail All The Various Processes Involved

Buying Options

Buying an options contract is in practice no different from buying stock. You are taking a long position on that option, expecting it to go up in value. You can buy options contracts by simply choosing exactly what you wish to buy and how many, and then placing a buy to open order with a broker. This order was named as such because you are opening a position through buying options.

If your options do go up in value, then you can either sell them or exercise your option depending on what suits you best. We provide more information on selling and exercising options later. One of the big advantages of options contracts is that you can buy them in situations when you expect the underlying asset to go up in value and also in situations when you expect the underlying asset to go down.

If you were expecting an underlying asset to go up in value, then you would buy call options, which gives you the right to buy the underlying asset at a fixed price. If you were expecting an underlying asset to go down in value, then you would buy put options, which gives you the right to sell the underlying asset at a fixed price. This is just one example of the flexibility on these contracts; there are several more.

If you have previously opened a short position on options contracts by writing them, then you can also buy those contracts back to close that position. To close a position by buying contracts you would place a buy to close order with your broker.

Selling & Writing Options

There are two ways in which you can sell options contracts. First, if you have previously bought contracts and wish to realize your profits, or cut your losses, then you would sell them by placing a sell to close order. The order is named as such because you are closing your position by selling options contracts. You would usually use that order if the options you owned had gone up in value and you wanted to take your profits at that point, or if the options you owned had fallen in value and you wanted to exit your position before incurring any other losses.

The other way you can sell options is by opening a short position and short selling them. This is also known as writing options because the process involves writing new contracts to be sold in the market. When you do this you are taking on the obligation in the contract i.e. if the holder chooses to exercise their option then you would have to sell them the underlying security at the strike price (if a call option) or buy the underlying security from them at the strike price (if a put option).

Writing options is done by using the sell to open order, and you would receive a payment at the time of placing such an order. This is generally riskier than trading through buying and then selling, but there are profits to be made if you know what you are doing. You would usually place such an order if you believed the relevant underlying security would not move in such a way that the holder would be able to exercise their option for a profit.

For example, if you believed that a particular stock was going to either remain static or fall in value, then you could choose to write and sell call options based on that stock. You would be liable to potential losses if the stock did go up in value, but if it failed to do so by the time the options expired you would keep the payment you received for writing them.

Exercising Options

Options traders tend to make their profits through the buying, selling, and writing of options rather than ever actually exercising them. However, depending on the strategies you are using and the reasons you have bought certain contracts, there may be occasions when you choose to exercise your options to buy or sell the underlying security. The simple fact that you can potentially make money out of exercising as well as buying and selling them further serves to illustrate just how much flexibility and versatility this form of trading offers.

Options Spreads

What makes trading options such an interesting way to invest is the ability to create options spreads. You can certainly make money trading by buying options and then selling them if you make a profit, but it's the spreads that are the seriously powerful tools in trading. A spread is quite simply when you enter a position on two or more options contracts based on the same underlying security; for example, buying options on a specific stock and also writing contracts on the same stock.

There are many different types of spreads that you can create, and they can be used for many different reasons. Most commonly, they have used to either limit the risk involved with taking a position or reducing the financial outlay required by taking a position. Most options trading strategies involve the use of spreads. Some strategies can be very complicated, but several fairly basic strategies are easy to understand.

The Value Of Options

The worth of a particular options contract to a buyer or seller is measured by its likelihood to meet their expectations. In the language of options, that's determined by whether or not the option is, or is likely to be, in-the-money or out-of-the-money at expiration. A call option is in-the-money if the current market value of the underlying stock is above the exercise price of the option. The call option is out-of-the-money if the stock is below the exercise price. A put option is in-the-money if the current market value of the underlying stock is below the exercise price. A put option is out-of-the-money if its underlying price is above the exercise price. If an option is not in-the-money at expiration, the option is assumed worthless.

An option's premium can have two parts: an intrinsic value and a time value. Intrinsic value is the amount that the option is in-the-money. Time value is the difference between the intrinsic value and the premium. In general, the longer time that market conditions work to your benefit, the greater the time value.

Options Prices

Several factors affect the price of an option. Supply and demand in the market where the option is traded is a large factor. This is also the case with an individual stock. The status of overall markets and the economy at large are broad influences. Specific influences include the identity of the underlying instrument, the instrument's traditional behavior, and current behavior. The instrument's volatility is also an important factor used to gauge the likelihood that an option will move in-the-money.

Benefits Of Trading Options

There are several benefits this form of trading offers, plus the versatility that we have referred to above. It's continuing to grow in popularity, not just with professional traders but also with more casual traders as well. Transactions generally require less capital than equivalent stock transactions. They may return smaller dollar figures but a potentially greater percentage of the investment than equivalent stock transactions.

Even investors who use options in speculative strategies such as writing uncovered calls don't usually realize dramatic returns. The potential profit is limited to the premium received for the contract. The potential loss is often unlimited. While leverage means the percentage returns can be significant, the amount of cash required is smaller than equivalent stock transactions. Although options may not be appropriate for all investors, they're among the most flexible of investment choices. Depending on the contract, options can protect or enhance the portfolios of many different kinds of investors in rising, falling, and neutral markets.

Reducing Your Risk

For many investors, options are useful tools for risk management. They act as insurance policies against a drop in stock prices. For example, if an investor is concerned that the price of their shares in LMN Corporation is about to drop, they can purchase puts that give the right to sell the stock at the strike price, no matter how low the market price drops before expiration. At the cost of the option's premium, the investor has insured themselves against losses below the strike price. This type of option practice is also known as hedging.

While hedging with options may help manage risk, it's important to remember that all investments carry some risk. Returns are never guaranteed. Investors who use options to manage risk look for ways to limit a potential loss. They may choose to purchase options since the loss is limited to the price paid for the premium. In return, they gain the right to buy or sell the underlying security at an acceptable price. They can also profit from a rise in the value of the option's premium if they choose to sell it back to the market rather than exercise it. Since writers of options are sometimes forced into buying or selling the stock at an unfavorable price, the risk associated with certain short positions may be higher.

Many options strategies are designed to minimize risk by hedging existing portfolios. While options act as safety nets, they're not risk-free. Since transactions usually open and close in the short term, gains can be realized quickly. Losses can mount as quickly as gains. It's important to understand the risks associated with holding, writing, and trading options before you include them in your investment portfolio.

Risking Your Principal

Like other securities including stocks, bonds, and mutual funds, options carry no guarantees. Be aware that it's possible to lose the entire principal invested, and sometimes more. As the holder of an option, you risk the entire amount of the premium you pay. But as an options writer, you take on a much higher level of risk. For example, if you write an uncovered call, you face unlimited potential loss, since there is no cap on how high a stock price can rise.

Since initial options investments usually require less capital than equivalent stock positions, your potential cash losses as an options investor are usually smaller than if you'd bought the underlying stock or sold the stock short. The exception to this general rule occurs when you use options to provide leverage. Percentage returns are often high, but percentage losses can be high as well.

What Are Options?

While traders can base an option contract on virtually any tradable asset, the most common come in two forms:

- ❖ Commodities option, trading tangible assets and raw materials;
- ❖ Stock options, trading shares of a corporation.

In an option contract, you have the right to either buy or sell an underlying asset at a specific price and date. At the expiration date your profits, if any, come from the difference between the asset's current market price and the price listed in your contract. This is why option contracts are called derivatives because they derive their value from an underlying asset.

The value of the contract comes, in large part, from the fact that you can choose to make this transaction only if it's profitable at the expiration date. For example, say you have an option contract to buy 1,000 ounces of coffee on Jan. 1 for $1.10 per ounce. On

Jan. 1, when this contract expires, you can either choose to exercise it or not, depending on whether it's profitable.

How An Option Contract Works

Every options contract has four specific components:

- ❖ Asset: The underlying asset being traded and in what quantity.
- ❖ Expiration Date: The date on which the contract expires.
- ❖ Strike Price: The price at which you trade the contract's underlying asset on the expiration date.
- ❖ Contract: The position of the option contract, whether a put or a call.

So, in our sample contract, we would have the following elements:

- ❖ Asset: 1,000 ounces of coffee
- ❖ Expiration Date: Jan. 1
- ❖ Strike Price: $1.10
- ❖ Contract: A put contract

This sample contract would give you the right to buy 1,000 ounces of coffee on Jan. 1 for $1.10 per ounce. Say that on January 1 the price of coffee has gone up to $1.20 per ounce, a difference of $0.10. You would make $100 (1,000 ounces times $0.10).

Options Can Resolve In Two Different Ways

Physical Settlement: Under this contract, you have the right to buy or sell the underlying asset. For example, in our sample contract involving coffee beans, a physical settlement contract would have you buying 1,000 ounces of coffee beans at the time of the contract's expiration. This is uncommon with commodities but very common with stock options.

Cash Resolution: In a cash resolution, traders don't exchange the underlying assets. Instead, when a contract expires, traders exchange the cash value of the underlying assets. So, in our sample involving coffee beans, if you exercised your option at the contract's expiration date you would receive a payment based on the difference between the contract's price and the current price of coffee.

Contract Specifications

A financial option is a contract between two counterparties with the terms of the option specified in a term sheet. Option contracts may be quite complicated; however, at minimum, they usually contain the following specifications:

- ❖ Whether the option holder has the right to buy (a call option) or the right to sell (a put option)
- ❖ The quantity and class of the underlying asset(s) (e.g., 100 shares of xyz co. B stock)

- The strike price, also known as the exercise price, which is the price at which the underlying transaction will occur upon exercise
- The expiration date, or expiry, which is the last date the option can be exercised
- The settlement terms, for instance, whether the writer must deliver the actual asset on exercise, or may simply tender the equivalent cash amount
- The terms by which the option is quoted in the market to convert the quoted price into the actual premium – the total amount paid by the holder to the writer

Profits And Premiums

The price of an option contract is called its "premium." Traders set an option's premium based on how likely they think it is that the contract will expire in the money, and based on how many units of the underlying asset the contract represents.

For example, our coffee contract might have a premium of $0.05 per ounce. This means that you would have to pay $50 ($0.05 times 1,000) to buy the contract.

Ultimately, options are a bet between two traders about how prices will move. When someone sells a call option, it's because they think that the price of this asset will stay below the contract's strike price. When they sell a put option, they believe that the asset's price will stay above it. In either case, they set their premium based on how likely they think this is. The higher the premium, the more likely they think it is that the contract will expire in the money.

Long Shot Contracts, On The Other Hand, Tend To Sell Quite Cheaply

As a trader, your profits are based on the difference between how much the contract cost and how much you made off it. Say you entered the contract to buy coffee for $1.10 on January 1, with a premium of $0.05 per ounce. If coffee costs $1.30 on the expiration date you'd profit $0.15 per ounce (the $0.20 difference between contract and market, minus the premium cost of $0.05).

Premiums are an up-front cost. If you don't exercise your contract at all, they are simply lost. However, that's also the extent of your losses. You can't lose more on an option contract than it cost upfront. The premium of the option (its price) is determined by intrinsic value plus its time value (extrinsic value).

Historical vs. Implied Volatility

Volatility in options trading refers to how large the price swings are for a given stock. Just as you would imagine, high volatility with securities (like stocks) means higher risk - and conversely, low volatility means lower risk. When trading options on the stock market, stocks with high volatility (ones whose share prices fluctuate a lot) are more expensive than those with low volatility (although due to the erratic nature of the stock market, even low volatility stocks can become high volatility ones eventually).

Common Options Trading Mistakes

There are plenty of mistakes even seasoned traders can make when trading options.

One common mistake for traders to make is that they think they need to hold on to their call or put option until the expiration date. If your option's underlying stock goes way up overnight (doubling your call or put option's value), you can exercise the contract immediately to reap the gains (even if you have, say, 29 days left for the option).

Another common mistake for options traders (especially beginners) is to fail to create a good exit plan for your option. For example, you may want to plan to exit your option when you either suffer a loss or when you've reached a profit that is to your liking (instead of holding out in your contract until the expiration date).

Still, other traders can make the mistake of thinking that cheaper is better. For options, this isn't necessarily true. The cheaper an option's premium is, the more "out of the money" the option typically is, which can be a riskier investment with less profit potential if it goes wrong. Buying "out of the money" call or put options means you want the underlying security to drastically change in value, which isn't always predictable.

Historical volatility is a good measure of volatility since it measures how much a stock fluctuated day-to-day over one year. On the other hand, implied volatility is an estimation of the volatility of a stock (or security) in the future based on the market over the time of the option contract.

Value: Time Value And In/At/Out Of The Money

If you are buying an option that is already "in the money" (meaning the option will immediately be in profit), its premium will have an extra cost because you can sell it immediately for a profit. On the other hand, if you have an option that is "at the money," the option is equal to the current stock price. And, as you may have guessed, an option that is "out of the money" is one that won't have additional value because it is currently not in profit.

For call options, "in the money" contracts will be those whose underlying asset's price (stock, ETF, etc.) is above the strike price. For put options, the contract will be "in the money" if the strike price is below the current price of the underlying asset (stock, ETF, etc.). The time value, which is also called the extrinsic value, is the value of the option above the intrinsic value (or, above the "in the money" area). If an option (whether a put or call option) is going to be "out of the money" by its expiration date, you can sell options to collect a time premium.

The longer an option has before its expiration date, the more time it has to make a profit, so its premium (price) is going to be higher because its time value is higher. Conversely, the less time an options contract has before it expires, the less its time value will be (the less additional time value will be added to the premium).

So, in other words, if an option has a lot of time before it expires, the more additional time value will be added to the premium (price) - and the less time it has before expiration, the less time value will be added to the premium.

Types Of Options

Many different types of options can be traded and these can be categorized in several ways. In a very broad sense, there are two main types: calls and puts. Calls give the buyer the right to buy the underlying asset, while puts give the buyer the right to sell the underlying asset. Along with this clear distinction, options are also usually classified based on whether they are American style or European style. This has nothing to do with geographical location, but rather when the contracts can be exercised. You can read more about the differences below.

Options can be further categorized based on the method in which they are traded, their expiration cycle, and the underlying security they relate to. There are also other specific types and several exotic options that exist. On this page, we have published a comprehensive list of the most common categories along with the different types that fall into these categories. We have also provided further information on each type.

- ❖ Calls
- ❖ Puts
- ❖ American Style
- ❖ European Style
- ❖ Exchange-Traded Options
- ❖ Over The Counter Options
- ❖ Option Type by Expiration
- ❖ Option Type by Underlying Security
- ❖ Employee Stock Options
- ❖ Cash Settled Options
- ❖ Exotic Options

1. Calls: Call options are contracts that give the owner the right to buy the underlying asset in the future at an agreed price. You would buy a call if you believed that the underlying asset was likely to increase in price over a given period. Calls have an expiration date and, depending on the terms of the contract, the underlying asset can be bought any time before the expiration date or on the expiration date.

2. Puts: Put options are essentially the opposite of calls. The owner of a put has the right to sell the underlying asset in the future at a pre-determined price. Therefore, you would buy a put if you were expecting the underlying asset to fall in value. As with calls, there is an expiration date in the contact.

3. American Style: The term "American style" about options has nothing to do with where contracts are bought or sold, but rather to the terms of the contracts. Options contracts come with an expiration date, at which point the owner has the right to buy the underlying security (if a call) or sell it (if a put). With American style options, the owner of the contract also has the right to exercise at any time before the expiration date. This additional flexibility is an obvious advantage to the owner of an American style contract.

4. European Style: The owners of European style options contracts are not afforded the same flexibility as with American style contracts. If you own a European style contract then you have the right to buy or sell the underlying asset on which the contract is based only on the expiration date and not before.

5. Exchange-Traded Options: Also known as listed options, this is the most common form of options. The term "Exchanged Traded" is used to describe an options contract that is listed on a public trading exchange. They can be bought and sold by anyone by using the services of a suitable broker. Exchange-traded options (also called "listed options") are a class of exchange-traded derivatives. Exchange-traded options have standardized contracts and are settled through a clearing house with fulfillment guaranteed by The Options Clearing Corporation (OCC). Since the contracts are standardized, accurate pricing models are often available. Exchange-traded options include:

- ❖ Stock options
- ❖ Bond options and other interest rate options
- ❖ Stock market index options or, simply, index options and
- ❖ Options on futures contracts
- ❖ Callable bull/bear contract

6. Over The Counter Options: "Over The Counter" (OTC) options are only traded in the OTC markets, making them less accessible to the general public. They tend to be customized contracts with more complicated terms than most Exchange Traded contracts. Over-the-counter options (OTC options, also called "dealer options") are traded between two private parties and are not listed on an exchange. The terms of an OTC option are unrestricted and may be individually tailored to meet any business need. In general, the option writer is a well-capitalized institution (to prevent credit risk). Option types commonly traded over the counter include:

- ❖ Interest rate options
- ❖ Currency cross rate options, and
- ❖ Options on swaps or swaptions.

By avoiding an exchange, users of OTC options can narrowly tailor the terms of the option contract to suit individual business requirements. Also, OTC option transactions generally do not need to be advertised to the market and face little or no regulatory requirements. However, OTC counterparties must establish credit lines with each other, and conform to each other's clearing and settlement procedures. With few exceptions, there are no secondary markets for employee stock options. These must either be exercised by the original grantee or allowed to expire.

7. Exchange Trading: The most common way to trade options is via standardized options contracts that are listed by various futures and options exchanges. Listings and prices are tracked and can be looked up by ticker symbol. By publishing continuous, live markets for option prices, an exchange enables independent parties to engage in price discovery and execute transactions. As an intermediary to both sides of the transaction, the benefits the exchange provides to the transaction include:

❖ Fulfillment of the contract is backed by the credit of the exchange, which typically has the highest rating (AAA),

❖ Counterparties remain anonymous,

❖ Enforcement of market regulation to ensure fairness and transparency, and

❖ Maintenance of orderly markets, especially during fast trading conditions.

8. Option Type by Underlying Security: When people use the term options they are generally referring to stock options, where the underlying asset shares in a publically listed company. While these are certainly very common, there are also several other types where the underlying security is something else. We have listed the most common of these below with a brief description.

1. Stock Options: The underlying asset for these contracts is shared in a specific publically listed company.

2. Index Options: These are very similar to stock options, but rather than the underlying security stocking in a specific company it is an index – such as the S&P 500.

3. Forex/Currency Options: Contracts of this type grant the right to buy or sell a specific currency at an agreed exchange rate.

4. Futures Options: The underlying security for this type is a specified futures contract. A futures option essentially gives the owner the right to enter into that specified futures contract.

5. Commodity Options: The underlying asset for a contract of this type can be either a physical commodity or a commodity futures contract.

6. Basket Options: A basket contract is based on the underlying asset of a group of securities which could be made up of stocks, currencies, commodities, or other financial instruments.

9. Option Type By Expiration: Contracts can be classified by their expiration cycle, which relates to the point to which the owner must exercise their right to buy or sell the relevant asset under the terms of the contract. Some contracts are only available with one specific type of expiration cycle, while with some contracts you can choose. For most options traders, this information is far from essential, but it can help to recognize the terms. Below are some details on the different contract types based on their expiration cycle.

1. Regular Options: These are based on the standardized expiration cycles that options contracts are listed under. When purchasing a contract of this type, you will have the choice of at least four different expiration months to choose from. The reasons for these expiration cycles existing in the way they do is due to restrictions put in place when options were first introduced about when they could be traded. Expiration cycles can get somewhat complicated, but all you need to understand is that you will be able to choose your preferred expiration date from a selection of at least four different months.

2. Weekly Options: Also known as weeklies, these were introduced in 2005. They are currently only available on a limited number of underlying securities, including some of the major indices, but their popularity is increasing. The basic principle of weeklies is the same as regular options, but they just have a much shorter expiration period.

3. Quarterly Options: Also referred to as quarterlies, these are listed on the exchanges with expirations for the nearest four quarters plus the final quarter of the following year. Unlike regular contracts that expire on the third Friday of the expiration month, quarterlies expire on the last day of the expiration month.

4. Long-Term Expiration Anticipation Securities: These longer-term contracts are generally known as LEAPS and are available on a fairly wide range of underlying securities. LEAPS always expire in January but can be bought with expiration dates for the following three years.

10. Employee Stock Options: These are a form of stock option where employees are granted contracts based on the stock of the company they work for. They are generally used as a form of remuneration, bonus, or incentive to join a company.

11. Exotic Options: The exotic option is a term that is used to apply to a contract that has been customized with more complex provisions. They are also classified as Non-Standardized options. There are a plethora of different exotic contracts, many of which are only available from OTC markets. Some exotic contracts, however, are becoming more popular with mainstream investors and getting listed on the public exchanges. Below are some of the more common types.

1. Barrier Options: These contracts provide a pay-out to the holder if the underlying security does (or does not, depending on the terms of the contract) reach a pre-determined price.

2. Binary Options: When a contract of this type expires in profit for the owner, they are awarded a fixed amount of money.

3. Choose Options: These were named "Chooser," options because they allow the owner of the contract to choose whether it's a call or a put when a specific date is reached.

4. Compound Options: These are options where the underlying security is another option contract.

5. Look Back Options: This type of contract has no strike price but instead allows the owner to exercise at the best price the underlying security reached during the term of the contract.

Options Risk Metrics: The Greeks

The "Greeks" is a term used in the options market to describe the different dimensions of risk involved in taking an options position, either in a particular option or a portfolio of options. These variables are called Greeks because they are typically associated with Greek symbols. Each risk variable is a result of an imperfect assumption or relationship of the option with another underlying variable. Traders use different Greek values, such as delta, theta, and others, to assess options risk and manage option portfolios.

Delta

Delta (Δ) represents the rate of change between the option's price and a $1 change in the underlying asset's price. In other words, the price sensitivity of the option relative to the underlying. Delta of a call option has a range between zero and one, while the delta of a put option has a range between zero and a negative one. For example, assume an investor is long a call option with a delta of 0.50. Therefore, if the underlying stock increases by $1, the option's price would theoretically increase by 50 cents.

For options traders, delta also represents the hedge ratio for creating a delta-neutral position. For example, if you purchase a standard American call option with a 0.40 delta, you will need to sell 40 shares of stock to be fully hedged. Net delta for a portfolio of options can also be used to obtain the portfolio's hedge ration.

A less common usage of an option's delta is it's the current probability that it will expire in-the-money. For instance, a 0.40 delta call option today has an implied 40% probability of finishing in-the-money.

Theta

Theta (Θ) represents the rate of change between the option price and time, or time sensitivity - sometimes known as an option's time decay. Theta indicates the amount an option's price would decrease as the time to expiration decreases, all else equal. For example, assume an investor is long an option with a theta of -0.50. The option's price would decrease by 50 cents every day that passes, all else being equal. If three trading days pass, the option's value would theoretically decrease by $1.50.

Theta increases when options are at-the-money, and decreases when options are in- and out-of-the-money. Options closer to expiration also have accelerating time decay. Long calls and long puts will usually have negative Theta; short calls and short puts will have positive Theta. By comparison, an instrument whose value is not eroded by time, such as a stock, would have zero Theta.

Gamma

Gamma (Γ) represents the rate of change between an option's delta and the underlying asset's price. This is called second-order (second-derivative) price sensitivity. Gamma indicates the amount the delta would change given a $1 move in the underlying security. For example, assume an investor is a long one call option on hypothetical stock XYZ. The call option has a delta of 0.50 and a gamma of 0.10. Therefore, if stock XYZ increases or decreases by $1, the call option's delta would increase or decrease by 0.10.

Gamma is used to determine how stable an option's delta is: higher gamma values indicate that delta could change dramatically in response to even small movements in the underlying's price. Gamma is higher for options that are at-the-money and lower for options that are in- and out-of-the-money and accelerates in magnitude as expiration approaches. Gamma values are generally smaller the further away from the date of expiration; options with longer expirations are less sensitive to delta changes. As expiration approaches, gamma values are typically larger, as price changes have more impact on gamma. Options traders may opt to not only hedge delta but also gamma to be delta-gamma neutral, meaning that as the underlying price moves, the delta will remain close to zero.

Vega

Vega (V) represents the rate of change between an option's value and the underlying asset's implied volatility. This is the option's sensitivity to volatility. Vega indicates the amount of an option's price changes given a 1% change in implied volatility. For example, an option with a Vega of 0.10 indicates the option's value is expected to change by 10 cents if the implied volatility changes by 1%.

Because increased volatility implies that the underlying instrument is more likely to experience extreme values, a rise in volatility will correspondingly increase the value of an option. Conversely, a decrease in volatility will negatively affect the value of the option. Vega is at its maximum for at-the-money options that have longer times until expiration.

Those familiar with the Greek language will point out that there is no actual Greek letter named vega. There are various theories about how this symbol, which resembles the Greek letter nu, found its way into stock-trading lingo.

Rho

Rho (p) represents the rate of change between an option's value and a 1% change in the interest rate. This measures sensitivity to the interest rate. For example, assume a call option has a rho of 0.05 and a price of $1.25. If interest rates rise by 1%, the value of the call option would increase to $1.30, all else being equal. The opposite is true for put options. Rho is greatest for at-the-money options with long times until expiration.

Minor Greeks

Some other Greeks, with aren't discussed as often, are lambda, epsilon, comma, vera, speed, zomma, color, ultima.

These Greeks are second- or third-derivatives of the pricing model and affect things such as the change in delta with a change in volatility and so on. They are increasingly used in options trading strategies as computer software can quickly compute and account for these complex and sometimes esoteric risk factors.

Risk And Profits From Buying Call Options

As mentioned earlier, the call options let the holder buy an underlying security at the stated strike price by the expiration date called the expiry. The holder has no obligation to buy the asset if they do not want to purchase the asset. The risk to the call option buyer is limited to the premium paid. Fluctuations of the underlying stock have no impact.

Call options buyers are bullish on a stock and believe the share price will rise above the strike price before the option's expiry. If the investor's bullish outlook is realized and the stock price increases above the strike price, the investor can exercise the option, buy the stock at the strike price, and immediately sell the stock at the current market price for a profit.

Their profit on this trade is the market share price less the strike share price plus the expense of the option the premium and any brokerage commission to place the orders. The result would be multiplied by the number of option contracts purchased, then multiplied by 100 assuming each contract represents 100 shares. However, if the underlying stock price does not move above the strike price by the expiration date, the option expires worthlessly. The holder is not required to buy the shares but will lose the premium paid for the call.

Risk And Profits From Selling Call Options

Selling call options is known as writing a contract. The writer receives the premium fee. In other words, an option buyer will pay the premium to the writer or seller of an option. The maximum profit is the premium received when selling the option. An investor who sells a call option is bearish and believes the underlying stock's price will fall or remain relatively close to the option's strike price during the life of the option.

If the prevailing market share price is at or below the strike price by expiry, the option expires worthlessly for the call buyer. The option seller pockets the premium as their profit. The option is not exercised because the option buyer would not buy the stock at the strike price higher than or equal to the prevailing market price.

However, if the market share price is more than the strike price at expiry, the seller of the option must sell the shares to an option buyer at that lower strike price. In other words, the seller must either sell shares from their portfolio holdings or buy the stock at the prevailing market price to sell to the call option buyer. The contract writer incurs a loss. How large of a loss depends on the cost basis of the shares they must use to cover the option order, plus any brokerage order expenses, but less any premium they received. As you can see, the risk to the call writers is far greater than the risk exposure of call buyers. The call buyer only loses the premium. The writer faces infinite risk because the stock price could continue to rise increasing losses significantly.

Risk And Profits From Buying Put Options

Put options are investments where the buyer believes the underlying stock's market price will fall below the strike price on or before the expiration date of the option. Once again, the holder can sell shares without the obligation to sell at the stated strike per-share price by the stated date.

Since buyers of put options want the stock price to decrease, the put option is profitable when the underlying stock's price is below the strike price. If the prevailing market price is less than the strike price at expiry, the investor can exercise the put. They will sell shares at the option's higher strike price. Should they wish to replace their holding of these shares they may buy them on the open market.

Their profit on this trade is the strike price less than the current market price, plus expenses the premium and any brokerage commission to place the orders. The result would be multiplied by the number of option contracts purchased, then multiplied by 100 assuming each contract represents 100 shares. The value of holding a put option will increase as the underlying stock price decreases. Conversely, the value of the put option declines as the stock price increases. The risk of buying put options is limited to the loss of the premium if the option expires worthlessly.

Risk And Profits From Selling Put Options

Selling put options is also known as writing a contract. A put option writer believes the underlying stock's price will stay the same or increase over the life of the option making them bullish on the shares. Here, the option buyer has the right to make the seller, buy shares of the underlying asset at the strike price on expiry.

If the underlying stock's price closes above the strike price by the expiration date, the put option expires worthlessly. The writer's maximum profit is the premium. The option isn't exercised because the option buyer would not sell the stock at the lower strike share price when the market price is more.

However, if the stock's market value falls below the option strike price, the put option writer is obligated to buy shares of the underlying stock at the strike price. In other words, the put option will be exercised by the option buyer. The buyer will sell their shares at the strike price since it is higher than the stock's market value. The risk for the put option writer happens when the market's price falls below the strike price. Now, at expiration, the seller is forced to purchase shares at the strike price. Depending on how much the shares have appreciated, the put writer's loss can be significant.

The put writer the seller can either hold on to the shares and hope the stock price rises back above the purchase price or sell the shares and take the loss. However, any loss is offset somewhat by the premium received. Sometimes an investor will write put options at a strike price that is where they see the shares being a good value and would be willing to buy at that price. When the price falls, and the option buyer exercises their option, they get the stock at the price they want, with the added benefit of receiving the option premium.

Chapter 2 - How Options Trading Works

What Are Options?

An option is a contract that allows (but doesn't require) an investor to buy or sell an underlying instrument like a security, ETF, or even index at a predetermined price over a certain period. Buying and selling options are done on the options market, which trades contracts based on securities. Buying an option that allows you to buy shares at a later time is called a "call option," whereas buying an option that allows you to sell shares at a later time is called a "put option."

However, options are not the same thing as stocks because they do not represent ownership in a company. And, although futures use contracts just like options do, options are considered a lower risk because you can withdraw (or walk away from) an options contract at any point. The price of the option (it's premium) is thus a percentage of the underlying asset or security.

How Options Work

In terms of valuing option contracts, it is essentially all about determining the probabilities of future price events. The more likely something is to occur, the more expensive an option would be that profits from that event. For instance, a call value goes up as the stock (underlying) goes up. This is the key to understanding the relative value of options.

The less time there is until expiry, the less value an option will have. This is because the chances of a price move in the underlying stock diminish as we draw closer to expiry. This is why an option is a wasting asset. If you buy a one-month option that is out of the money, and the stock doesn't move, the option becomes less valuable with each passing day. Since time is a component to the price of an option, a one-month option is going to be less valuable than a three-month option. This is because with more time available, the probability of a price move in your favor increases, and vice versa.

Accordingly, the same option strike that expires in a year will cost more than the same strike for one month. This wasting feature of options is a result of time decay. The same option will be worthless tomorrow than it is today if the price of the stock doesn't move.

Volatility also increases the price of an option. This is because uncertainty pushes the odds of an outcome higher. If the volatility of the underlying asset increases, larger price swings increase the possibilities of substantial moves both up and down. Greater price swings will increase the chances of an event occurring. Therefore, the greater the volatility, the greater the price of the option. Options trading and volatility are intrinsically linked to each other in this way.

How Does An Option Work?

Options are derivative instruments, meaning that their prices are derived from the price of their underlying security, which could be almost anything: stocks, bonds, currencies, indexes, commodities, etc. Many options are created in a standardized form and traded on an options exchange like the Chicago Board Options Exchange (CBOE), although the two parties to an options contract can agree to create options with completely customized terms.

There are two types of options: call options and put options. A buyer of a call option has the right to buy the underlying asset for a certain price. The buyer of a put option has the right to sell the underlying asset for a certain price.

Here's A Brief Look At A Few Of The Most Common Types Of Options:

Every option represents a contract between the options writer and the buyer of the options.

1. The options writer is the party that "writes," or creates, the options contract, and then sells it. If the investor who buys the contract chooses to exercise the option, the writer is obligated to fulfill the transaction by buying or selling the underlying asset,

depending on the type of option he wrote. If the buyer chooses to not exercise the option, the writer does nothing and gets to keep the premium (the price the option was originally sold for).

2. The options buyer has a lot of power in this relationship. He chooses whether or not they will complete the transaction. When the option expires, if the buyer doesn't want to exercise the option, he doesn't have to. The buyer has purchased the option to carry out a certain transaction in the future -- hence the name.

An Example of How Options Work

Now that you know the basics of options, here is an example of how they work. We'll use a fictional firm called Cory's Tequila Company.

Let's say that on May 1st, the stock price of Cory's Tequila Co. is $67 and the premium (cost) is $3.15 for a July 70 Call, which indicates that the expiration is the 3rd Friday of July and the strike price is $70. The total price of the contract is $3.15 x 100 = $315. In reality, you'd also have to take commissions into account, but we'll ignore them for this example.

Remember, a stock option contract is the option to buy 100 shares; that's why you must multiply the contract by 100 to get the total price. The strike price of $70 means that the stock price must rise above $70 before the call option is worth anything;

furthermore, because the contract is $3.15 per share, the break-even price would be $73.15.

When the stock price is $67, it's less than the $70 strike price, so the option is worthless. But don't forget that you've paid $315 for the option, so you are currently down by this amount.

Three weeks later the stock price is $78. The options contract has increased along with the stock price and is now worth $8.25 x 100 = $825. Subtract what you paid for the contract, and your profit is ($8.25 - $3.15) x 100 = $510. You almost doubled our money in just three weeks! You could sell your options, which is called "closing your position," and take your profits—unless, of course, you think the stock price will continue to rise... Say we let it ride.

By the expiration date, the price tanks and is now $62. Because this is less than our $70 strike price and there is no time left, the option contract is worthless. We are now down to the original investment of $315.

To recap, here is what happened to our option investment:

Date	May 1st	May 21st	Expiry Date
Stock Price	$67	$78	$62
Call Price	$3.15	$8.25	worthless
Contract Value	$315	$825	$0

Paper Gain/Loss	$0	$510	-$315

The price swing for the length of this contract from high to low was $825, which would have given us over double our original investment. This is leverage in action.

Exercising Versus Selling

So far we've talked about options as the right to buy or sell the underlying. This is true, but in actuality, a majority of options are not exercised.

In our example, you could make money by exercising at $70 and then selling the stock back in the market at $78 for a profit of $8 a share. You could also keep the stock, knowing you were able to buy it at a discount to the present value.

However, the majority of the time holders choose to take their profits by selling (closing out) their position. This means that holders sell their options in the market, and writers buy their positions back to close. According to the CBOE, about 10% of options are exercised, 60% are closed out, and 30% expire worthlessly.

Intrinsic Value And Time Value

At this point, it is worth explaining more about the pricing of options. In our example, the premium (price) of the option went from $3.15 to $8.25. These fluctuations can be explained by intrinsic value and time value.

An option's premium is its intrinsic value + time value. Remember, intrinsic value is the amount in-the-money, which, for a call option, is the amount that the price of the stock is higher than the strike price. Time value represents the possibility of the option increasing in value. So, the price of the option in our example can be thought of as the following:

Premium = Intrinsic Value   +   Time Value

$8.25 = $8 + $0.25Premium ($8,25) = Intrinsic Value ($8) + Time Value ($0,25)

In real life options almost always trade above intrinsic value.

Why Does An Option Matter?

Investors use options for two primary reasons: to speculate and to hedge risk. Rational investors realize there is no "sure thing," as every investment incurs at least some risk. This risk is what the investor is compensated for when he or she purchases an asset. Hedging is like buying insurance. It is protection against unforeseen events, but you hope you never have to use it. Should a stock take an unforeseen turn, holding an option opposite of your position will help to limit your losses? If you'd like to read more in-depth information about options, check out these definitions:

❖ Call Option: Option to purchase the underlying asset.

❖ Put Option: Option to sell the underlying asset.

❖ Options Contract: The agreement between the writer and the buyer.

❖ Expiration Date: The last day an options contract can be exercised.

❖ Strike Price: The pre-determined price the underlying asset can be bought/sold for.

❖ Intrinsic Value: The current value of the option's underlying asset.

❖ Time Value: The additional amount that traders are willing to pay for an option.

❖ Vanilla Option: A normal option with no special features, terms, or conditions.

❖ American Option: Option that can be exercised any time before the expiration date.

❖ European Option: Option that can be exercised only on the expiration date.

❖ Exotic Option: Any option with a complex structure or payoff calculation.

Buying, Selling Calls/Puts

There are four things you can do with options:

- ❖ Buy calls
- ❖ Sell calls
- ❖ Buy puts
- ❖ Sell puts

Buying stock gives you a long position. Buying a call option gives you a potential long position in the underlying stock. Short-selling a stock gives you a short position. Selling a naked or uncovered call gives you a potential short position in the underlying stock.

Buying a put option gives you a potential short position in the underlying stock. Selling a naked, or unmarried, but gives you a potential long position in the underlying stock. Keeping these four scenarios straight is crucial.

People who buy options are called holders and those who sell options are called writers of options. Here is the important distinction between holders and writers:

1. Call holders and put holders (buyers) are not obligated to buy or sell. They have the choice to exercise their rights. This limits the risk of buyers of options to only the premium spent.

2. Call writers and put writers (sellers), however, are obligated to buy or sell if the option expires in-the-money (more on that below). This means that a seller may be required to make good on a promise to buy or sell. It also implies that option sellers have exposure to more, and in some cases, unlimited, risks. This means writers can lose much more than the price of the options premium.

Why Use Options

Speculation

Speculation is a wager on future price direction. A speculator might think the price of a stock will go up, perhaps based on fundamental analysis or technical analysis. A speculator might buy the stock or buy a call option on the stock. Speculating with a call option instead of buying the stock outright is attractive to some traders since options provide leverage. An out-of-the-money call option may only cost a few dollars or even cents compared to the full price of a $100 stock.

Hedging

Options were invented for hedging purposes. Hedging with options is meant to reduce risk at a reasonable cost. Here, we can think of using options like an insurance policy. Just as you insure your house or car, options can be used to ensure your investments against a downturn.

Imagine that you want to buy technology stocks. But you also want to limit losses. By using put options, you could limit your downside risk and cost-effectively enjoy all the upside. For short-sellers, call options can be used to limit losses if wrong especially during a short squeeze.

Chapter 3 - The Basics of Options Trading

The Basics of Trading Options Contracts

A financial option is a contractual agreement between two parties. Although some option contracts are over the counter, meaning they are between two parties without going through an exchange, standardized contracts known as listed options trade on exchanges. Options are a type of derivative security. An option is a derivative because its price is intrinsically linked to the price of something else. If you buy an options contract, it grants you the right, but not the obligation to buy or sell an underlying asset at a set price on or before a certain date. A call option gives the holder the right to buy a stock and a put option gives the holder the right to sell a stock. Think of a call option as a down-payment for a future purpose. Options contracts give the owner rights and the seller obligations. Here are the key definitions and details:

1. Call Option: A call option gives the owner (seller) the right (obligation) to buy (sell) a specific number of shares of the underlying stock at a specific price by a predetermined date. A call option allows you to profit from price gains in the underlying stock at a fraction of the cost of owning the stock.

A call is the option to buy the underlying stock at a predetermined price (the strike price) by a predetermined date (the expiry). The buyer of a call has the right to buy shares at the strike price until expiry. The seller of the call (also known as the call "writer") is the one with the obligation. If the call buyer decides to buy an act is known as exercising the option the call writer is obliged to sell his/her shares to the call buyer at the strike price.

So, say an investor bought a call option on Intel with a strike price at $20, expiring in two months. That call buyer has the right to exercise that option, paying $20 per share, and receiving the shares. The writer of the call would have the obligation to deliver those shares and be happy receiving $20 for them. We'll discuss the merits and motivations of each side of the trade momentarily.

2. Put Option: Put options give the owner (seller) the right (obligation) to sell (buy) a specific number of shares of the underlying stock at a specific price by a specific date. If you own put options on a stock that you own, and the price of the stock is falling, the put option is gaining in value, thus offsetting the losses on the stock and allowing you to make decisions about your stock ownership without panicking.

If a call is the right to buy, then perhaps unsurprisingly, a put is the option to sell the underlying stock at a predetermined strike price until a fixed expiry date. The put buyer has the right to sell shares at the strike price, and if he/she decides to sell, the put writer is obliged to buy at that price.

Investors who bought shares of Hewlett-Packard at the ouster of former CEO Carly Fiorina are sitting on some sweet gains over the past two years. And while they may believe that the company will continue to do well, perhaps, in the face of a potential economic slowdown, they're concerned about the company sliding with the rest of the market, and so buy a put option at the $40 strike to "protect" their gains. Buyers of the put have the right, until expiry, to sell their shares for $40. Sellers of the put must purchase the shares for $40 (which could hurt, if HP were to decline in price from here).

1. Rights Of The Owner Of An Options Contract: A call option gives the owner the right to buy a specific number of shares of stock at a predetermined price. A put option gives its owner the right to sell a specific number of shares of stock at a predetermined price.

2. Obligations Of An Options Seller: Sellers of call options have the obligation to sell a specific number of shares of the underlying stock at a predetermined price. Sellers of put options have the obligation to buy a specific amount of stock at a predetermined price.

To maximize your use of options, for both risk management and trading profits, make sure you understand the concepts put forth in each section fully before moving on. Focus on the option, consider how you might use it, and gauge the risk and reward associated with the option and the strategy. If you keep these factors in mind as you study each section, the concepts will be much easier to use as you move on to real-time trading.

Use Stock Options For The Following Objectives:

- ❖ To benefit from upside moves for less money
- ❖ To profit from downside moves in stocks without the risk of short selling
- ❖ To protect an individual stock position or an entire portfolio during periods of falling prices and market downturns

Always Be Aware Of The Risks Of Trading Options. Here Are Two Key Concepts:

1. Options contracts have a limited life. Each contract has an expiration date. That means if the move you anticipate is close to the expiration date, you will lose our entire initial investment. You can figure out how these things happen by paper trading before you do it in real-time. Paper trading lets you try different options for the underlying stock, accomplishing two things. One is that you can see what happens in real-time. Seeing what -happens, in turn, lets you figure out how to pick the best option and how to manage the position.

2. The wrong strategy can lead to disastrous results. If you take more risk than necessary, you will limit your rewards and expose yourself to unlimited losses. This is the same thing that would

happen if you sold stocks short, which would defeat the purpose of trading options. Options and specific option strategies let you accomplish the same thing as selling stocks short (profiting from a decrease in prices of the underlying asset) at a fraction of the cost.

Why Use Options?

A call buyer seeks to make a profit when the price of the underlying shares rises. The call price will rise as the shares do. The call writer is making the opposite bet, hoping for the stock price to decline or, at the very least, rise less than the amount received for selling the call in the first place.

The put buyer profits when the underlying stock price falls. A put increases in value as the underlying stock decreases in value. Conversely, put writers are hoping for the option to expire with the stock price above the strike price, or at least for the stock to decline an amount less than what they have been paid to sell the put.

We'll note here that relatively few options expire and see shares change hands. Options are, after all, tradable securities. As circumstances change, investors can lock in their profits (or losses) by buying (or selling) an opposite option contract to their original action.

Chapter 4 - Strike Price

Definition: The strike price is defined as the price at which the holder of an option can buy (in the case of a call option) or sell (in the case of a put option) the underlying security when the option is exercised. Hence, the strike price is also known as the exercise price.

What Is A Strike Price?

A strike price is a set price at which a derivative contract can be bought or sold when it is exercised. For call options, the strike price is where the security can be bought by the option holder; for put options, the strike price is the price at which the security can be sold.

The Strike Price Is Also Known As The Exercise Price.

The Exercise Price

An option buyer pays a price called a premium, which is the cost of the option, for their right to buy or sell the underlying asset at the option's strike price. If a buyer chooses to use that right, then they are "exercising" the option. In other words, the option's strike price is synonymous with its exercise price. Exercising an option is beneficial if the underlying asset price is above the strike price of the call option on it, or the underlying asset price is below the strike price of a put option.

Traders don't need to exercise the option. Exercising an option is not an obligation. You only exercise the option if you want to buy or sell the actual underlying asset. Most options are not exercised, even the profitable ones.

For example, a trader buys a call option for a premium of $1 on a stock with a strike price of $10. Near the expiration date of the option, the underlying stock is trading at $16. Instead of exercising the option and taking control of the stock at $10, the options trader will typically just sell the option, closing out the trade. In doing so, they net approximately $5 per share they control.

Since one option controls 100 shares of stock, this trades nets $500. The math is as follows: $16 share price less the strike price of $10 means the option is worth approximately $6. The trader paid $1 for the option; thus the profit is $5. The option is worth approximately $6 because other factors affect the worth of an option aside from the price of the underlying stock. These other factors are called greeks.

The strike price or exercise price is the price at which you take control of the underlying stock should you choose to exercise the option. Regardless of what price the underlying security is trading at, the strike price/exercise price is known when you buy the option contract, is fixed, and doesn't change for that specific option.

Facts: The strike price is the price at which a derivative contract can be bought or sold (exercised). Derivatives are financial products whose value is based (derived) on the underlying asset, usually another financial instrument. The strike price, also known as the exercise price, is the most important determinant of option value.

Understanding Strike Prices

Strike prices are used in derivatives (mainly options) trading. Derivatives are financial products whose value is based (derived) on the underlying asset, usually another financial instrument. The strike price is a key variable of call and puts options. For example, the buyer of a stock option call would have the right, but not the obligation, to buy that stock in the future at the strike price. Similarly, the buyer of a stock option put would have the right, but not the obligation, to sell that stock in the future at the strike price.

The strike. or exercise price, is the most important determinant of option value. Strike prices are established when a contract is first written. It tells the investor what price the underlying asset must reach before the option is in-the-money (ITM). Strike prices are standardized, meaning they are at fixed dollar amounts, such as $31, $32, $33, $102.50, $105, and so on.

The price difference between the underlying stock price and the strike price determines an option's value. For buyers of a call option, if the strike price is above the underlying stock price, the option is out of the money (OTM). In this case, the option doesn't have intrinsic value, but it may still have value based on volatility and time until expiration as either of these two factors could put the option in the money in the future. Conversely, If the underlying stock price is above the strike price, the option will have intrinsic value and be in the money.

A buyer of a put option will be in the money when the underlying stock price is below the strike price and be out of the money when the underlying stock price is above the strike price. Again, an OTM option won't have intrinsic value, but it may still have value based on the volatility of the underlying asset and the time left until option expiration.

How Strike Prices Work

Strike prices are fixed in the option contract. For call options, the option holder has the right to purchase the underlying stock at that strike price up to the expiration date. For put options, the strike price is the price at which the underlying stock can be sold.

For example, an investor purchases a call option contract on shares of ABC Company at a $5 strike price. Over the life of the option contract, the holder has the right to exercise the option and purchase 100 shares of ABC for $500. If the price of ABC shares rises to $10, the option holder can lock in a $500 profit by exercising the option because it allows him to buy shares at $5 and sell them for $10 in the open market.

Why Strike Prices Matter

The strike price is one of the most important elements of options pricing. At the expiration date, the difference between the stock's market price and the option's strike price represents the amount of profit gained by exercising the option.

Strike Price Example

Assume there are two option contracts. One is a call option with a $100 strike price. The other is a call option with a $150 strike price. The current price of the underlying stock is $145. Assume both call options are the same, the only difference is the strike price. At expiration, the first contract is worth $45. That is, it is in the money by $45. This is because the stock is trading $45 higher than the strike price.

The second contract is out of the money by $5. If the price of the underlying asset is below the call's strike price at expiration, the option expires worthless. If we have two put options, both about to expire, and one has a strike price of $40 and the other has a strike price of $50, we can look to the current stock price to see which option has value. If the underlying stock is trading at $45, the $50 put option has a $5 value. This is because the underlying stock is below the strike price of the put.

The $40 put option has no value because the underlying stock is above the strike price. Recall that put options allow the option buyer to sell at the strike price. There is no point in using the option to sell at $40 when they can sell at $45 in the stock market. Therefore, the $40 strike price put is worthless at expiration.

What Is The Strike Price?

The strike price is the price at which the holder of the option can exercise the option to buy or sell an underlying security, depending on whether they hold a call option or put option. An option is a contract where the option buyer purchases the right to exercise the contract at a specific price, which is known as the strike price.

Buying or selling options is a popular trading strategy. Options trading is not complex, but as with any other investment, having good information is important. In the image below, we can see the strike price for a call option, which confers the right to buy at the strike price and the break-even point where the option seller starts losing money.

Call Options – Strike Price

The buyer and the seller of a call option agreement, according to which the buyer gets the right to buy a specified number of shares of stock at a specified price and the seller receives the purchase price for the option in return for agreeing to sell the shares to the option holder at the strike price if the option holder elects to exercise their option. Options are only good for a set period, after which the option expires.

The buyer of the option can exercise the option at any time before the specified expiration date. If the call option expires "out-of-the-money", that is with the underlying stock price still below the option strike price, then the option seller will profit by the amount of money received for the sale of the option. If the option is "in the money" before expiratio meaning the underlying stock price has risen to a point above the strike price of the option – then the buyer will profit by the difference between the option strike price and the actual stock price, multiplied by the number of shares in the option. (Stock options are commonly for a lot of 100 shares.)

Put Options – Strike Price

Here, the buyer and the seller of an option also agree, according to which the option buyer can exercise the right to sell short shares of the stock at the option strike price. Again, the option seller receives the purchase price of the option, known as the "premium".

The buyer of a put option possesses the right, but not an obligation, to exercise the option and sell short the specified number of shares of stock to the option seller any time before the option expiry, at the predetermined exercise price. In this trade, the buyer of the option will profit if the stock price falls below the option strike price before the expiration. The seller will profit from selling the option if the option expires out of the money, which in the case of a put option means the stock price remains higher than the strike price up to the date of the option's expiration.

Strike Price, Option Premium & Moneyness

When selecting options to buy or sell, for options expiring in the same month, the option's price (aka premium) and moneyness depend on the option's strike price.

Relationship Between Strike Price & Call Option Price

For call options, the higher the strike price, the cheaper the option. The following table lists option premiums typical for near term call options at various strike prices when the underlying stock is trading at $50

Strike Price	Moneyness Call	Option Premium	Intrinsic Value	Time Value
35	ITM	$15.50	$15	$0.50
40	ITM	$11.25	$10	$1.25
45	ITM	$7	$5	$2
50	ATM	$4.50	$0	$4.50
55	OTM	$2.50	$0	$2.50
60	OTM	$1.50	$0	$1.50
65	OTM	$0.75	$0	$0.75

Relationship Between Strike Price & Put Option Price

Conversely, for put options, the higher the strike price, the more expensive the option. The following table lists option premiums typical for near term put options at various strike prices when the underlying stock is trading at $50

Strike Price	Moneyness Put	Option Premium	Intrinsic Value	Time Value
35	OTM	$0.75	$0	$0.75
40	OTM	$1.50	$0	$1.50
45	OTM	$2.50	$0	$2.50
50	ATM	$4.50	$0	$4.50
55	ITM	$7	$5	$2
60	ITM	$11.25	$10	$1.25
65	ITM	$15.50	$15	$0.50

Strike Price Intervals

The strike price intervals vary depending on the market price and asset type of the underlying. For lower-priced stocks (usually $25 or less), intervals are at 2.5 points. Higher priced stocks have strike price intervals of 5 points (or 10 points for very expensive stocks priced at $200 or more). Index options typically have strike price intervals of 5 or 10 points while futures options generally have strike intervals of around one or two points.

Chapter 5 - Covered Calls

A covered call refers to transaction in the financial market in which the investor selling call options owns the equivalent amount of the underlying security. To execute this an investor holding a long position in an asset then writes (sells) call options on that same asset to generate an income stream. The investor's long position in the asset is the "cover" because it means the seller can deliver the shares if the buyer of the call option chooses to exercise. If the investor simultaneously buys stock and writes call options against that stock position, it is known as a "buy-write" transaction.

A covered call is a popular options strategy used to generate income in the form of options premiums. To execute a covered call, an investor holding a long position in an asset then writes (sells) call options on that same asset. It is often employed by those who intends to hold the underlying stock for a long time but does not expect an appreciable price increase in the near term. This strategy is ideal for an investor who believes the underlying price will not move much over the near-term.

A covered call is a financial market transaction in which the seller of call options owns the corresponding amount of the underlying instrument, such as shares of a stock or other securities. If a trader buys the underlying instrument at the same time the trader sells the call, the strategy is often called a "buy-write" strategy. In equilibrium, the strategy has the same payoffs as writing a put option.

Understanding Covered Calls

Covered calls are a neutral strategy, meaning the investor only expects a minor increase or decrease in the underlying stock price for the life of the written call option. This strategy is often employed when an investor has a short-term neutral view on the asset and for this reason holds the asset long and simultaneously has a short position via the option to generate income from the option premium.

Simply put, if an investor intends to hold the underlying stock for a long time but does not expect an appreciable price increase in the near term then they can generate income (premiums) for their account while they wait out the lull. A covered call serves as a short-term hedge on a long stock position and allows investors to earn income via the premium received for writing the option. However, the investor forfeits stock gains if the price moves above the option's strike price. They are also obligated to provide 100 shares at the strike price (for each contract written) if the buyer chooses to exercise the option.

A covered call strategy is not useful for a very bullish nor a very bearish investor. If an investor is very bullish, they are typically better off not writing the option and just holding the stock. The option caps the profit on the stock, which could reduce the overall profit of the trade if the stock price spikes. Similarly, if an investor is very bearish, they may be better off simply selling the stock, since the premium received for writing a call option will do little to offset the loss on the stock if the stock plummets.

The long position in the underlying instrument is said to provide the "cover" as the shares can be delivered to the buyer of the call if the buyer decides to exercise. Writing (i.e. selling) a call generates income in the form of the premium paid by the option buyer. And if the stock price remains stable or increases, then the writer will be able to keep this income as a profit, even though the profit may have been higher if no call were written. The risk of stock ownership is not eliminated. If the stock price declines, then the net position will likely lose money.

A call option is a contract that gives the buyer the legal right (but not the obligation) to buy 100 shares of the underlying stock or one futures contract at the strike price any time on or before expiration. If the seller of the call option also owns the underlying security, the option is considered "covered" because he or she can deliver the instrument without purchasing it on the open market at possibly unfavorable pricing.

The covered call is a strategy employed by both new and experienced traders. Because it is a limited risk strategy, it is often used instead of writing calls "naked" and, therefore, brokerage firms do not place as many restrictions on the use of this strategy. You will need to be approved for options by your broker before using this strategy, and you will likely need to be specifically approved for covered calls. Read on as we cover this option strategy and show you how you can use it to your advantage.

Options Basics

A call option gives the buyer the right, but not the obligation, to buy the underlying instrument (in this case, a stock) at the strike price on or before the expiry date. For example, if you buy July 40 XYZ calls, you have the right, but not the obligation, to purchase XYZ at $40 per share any time between now and the July expiration. This type of option can be precious in the event of a significant move above $40. Each option contract you buy is for 100 shares. The amount the trader pays for the option is called the premium.

Options have an unfair reputation as being complex and reserved only for advanced traders, but as you'll learn in Investopedia Academy's Options for Beginners course, that isn't the case. With clear and concise explanations of what options are and how to use them in your favor, you'll quickly discover how options trading can take you where stocks can't.

There are two values to the option, the intrinsic and extrinsic value, or time premium. Using our XYZ example, if the stock is trading at $45, our July 40 calls have $5 of intrinsic value. If the calls are trading at $6, that extra dollar is the time premium. If the stock is trading at $38 and our option is trading at $2, the option only has a time premium and is said to be out of the money.

Option sellers write the option in exchange for receiving the premium from the option buyer. They are expecting the option to expire worthless and, therefore, keep the premium. For some traders, the disadvantage of writing options naked is the unlimited risk. When you are an option buyer, your risk is limited to the premium you paid for the option. But when you are a seller, you assume the significant risk.

Refer back to our XYZ example. The seller of that option has given the buyer the right to buy XYZ at 40. If the stock goes to 50 and the buyer exercises the option, the option seller will be selling XYZ at $40. If the seller does not own the underlying stock, he or she will have to buy it on the open market for $50 to sell it at $40. Clearly, the more the stock's price increases, the greater the risk for the seller.

How A Covered Call Can Help

In the covered call strategy, we are going to assume the role of the option seller. However, we are not going to assume unlimited risk because we will already own the underlying stock. This gives rise to the term "covered" call because you are covered against unlimited losses if the option goes in the money and is exercised.

The covered call strategy requires two steps. First, you already own the stock. It needn't be in 100 share blocks, but it will need to be at least 100 shares. You will then sell, or write, one call option for each multiple of 100 shares: 100 shares = 1 call, 200 shares = 2 calls, 226 shares = 2 calls, and so on.

When using the covered call strategy, you have slightly different risk considerations than you do if you own the stock outright. You do get to keep the premium you receive when you sell the option, but if the stock goes above the strike price, you have capped the amount you can make.

When To Use A Covered Call

There are several reasons traders employ covered calls. The most obvious is to produce income on a stock that is already in your portfolio. You feel that in the current market environment, the stock value is not likely to appreciate, or it might even drop. Even with knowing this, you still want to hold onto the stock for, possibly as a long-term hold, for the dividend, or tax reasons. As a result, you may decide to write covered calls against this position.

Alternatively, many traders look for opportunities on options they feel are overvalued and will offer a good return. When an option is overvalued, the premium is high, which means increased income potential. To enter a covered call position on a stock, you do not own; you should simultaneously buy the stock (or already own it) and sell the call. Remember when doing this that the stock may go down in value. While the option risk is limited by owning the stock, there is still risk in owning the stock directly.

What To Do At Expiration

Eventually, we will reach expiration day.

If the option is still out of the money, likely, it will just expire worthless and not be exercised. In this case, you don't need to do anything. You could then write another option against your stock if you wish.

If the option is in the money, expect the option to be exercised. Depending on your brokerage firm, everything is usually automatic when the stock is called away. Be aware of what fees will be charged in this situation, as each broker will be different. You will need to be aware of this so that you can plan appropriately when determining whether writing a given covered call will be profitable.

Let's look at a brief example. Suppose that you buy 100 shares of XYZ at $38 and sell the July 40 calls for $1. In this case, you would bring in $100 in premiums for the option you sold. This would make your cost basis on the stock $37 ($38 paid per share - $1 for the option premium received). If the July expiration arrives and the stock is trading at or below $40 per share, the option will likely expire worthless and you will keep the premium. You can then continue to hold the stock and write another option if you choose.

If, however, the stock is trading at $41, you can expect the stock to be called away. You will be selling it at $40, which is the option's strike price. But remember, you brought in $1 in premium for the option, so your profit on the trade will be $3 (bought the stock for $38, received $1 for the option, stock called away at $40). Likewise, if you had bought the stock and not sold the option, your profit in this example would be the same $3 (bought at $38, sold at $41). If the stock is higher than $41, the trader that held the stock and did not write the 40 call would be gaining more, whereas for the trader who wrote the 40 covered call the profits would be capped.

Profiting From Covered Calls

The buyer pays the seller of the call option a premium to obtain the right to buy shares or contracts at a predetermined future price. The premium is a cash fee paid on the day the option is sold and is the seller's money to keep, regardless of whether the option is exercised or not. A covered call is therefore most profitable if the stock moves up to the strike price, generating profit from the long stock position, while the call that was sold expires worthless, allowing the call writer to collect the entire premium from its sale.

When To Sell A Covered Call

When you sell a covered call, you get paid in exchange for giving up a portion of future upside. For example, let's assume you buy XYZ stock for $50 per share, believing it will rise to $60 within one year. You're also willing to sell at $55 within six months, giving up further upside while taking a short-term profit. In this scenario, selling a covered call on the position might be an attractive strategy.

The stock's option chain indicates that selling a $55 six-month call option will cost the buyer a $4 per share premium. You could sell that option against your shares, which you purchased at $50 and hope to sell at $60 within a year. Writing this covered call creates an obligation to sell the shares at $55 within six months if the underlying price reaches that level. You get to keep the $4 in premium plus the $55 from the share sale, for the total of $59, or an 18% return over six months.

Advantages Of Covered Calls

Selling covered call options can help offset downside risk or add to upside return, taking the cash premium in exchange for future upside beyond the strike price plus premium.during the contract period. In other words, if XYZ stock in the example closes above $59, the seller makes less money than if he or she simply held the stock. However, if the stock ends the six months below $59 per share, the seller makes more money or loses less money than if the options sale hadn't taken place.

Maximum Profit And Loss

The maximum profit of a covered call is equivalent to the strike price of the short call option, less the purchase price of the underlying stock, plus the premium received. The maximum loss is equivalent to the purchase price of the underlying stock less the premium received.

Risks Of Covered Calls

Call sellers have to hold onto underlying shares or contracts or they'll be holding naked calls, which have theoretically unlimited loss potential if the underlying security rises. Therefore, sellers need to buy back options positions before expiration if they want to sell shares or contracts, increasing transaction costs while lowering net gains or increasing net losses.

Risks Of Covered Call Writing

The risks of covered call writing have already been briefly touched on. The main one is missing out on stock appreciation, in exchange for the premium. If a stock skyrockets, because a call was written, the writer only benefits from the stock appreciation up to the strike price, but no higher. In strong upward moves, it would have been favorable to simple hold the stock, and not write the call. While a covered call is often considered a low-risk options strategy, that isn't necessarily true. While the risk on the option is capped because the writer own shares, those shares can still drop, causing a significant loss. Although, the premium income helps slightly offset that loss.

This brings up the third potential downfall. Writing the option is one more thing to monitor. It makes a stock trade slightly more complicated and involves more transactions and more commissions.

Risks And Rewards Of The Covered Call Options Strategy

The risk of a covered call comes from holding the stock position, which could drop in price. Your maximum loss occurs if the stock goes to zero. Therefore, you would calculate your maximum loss per share as:

Maximum Loss Per Share = Stock Entry Price - Option Premium Received

For example, if you buy a stock at $9, and receive a $0.10 option premium on your sold call, your maximum loss is $8.90 per share. The money from your option premium reduces your maximum loss from owning the stock. The option premium income comes at a cost though, as it also limits your upside on the stock. You can only profit on the stock up to the strike price of the options contracts you sold. Therefore, calculate your maximum profit as:

Maximum Profit = (Strike Price - Stock Entry Price) + Option Premium Received

For example, if you buy a stock at $9, receive a $0.10 option premium from selling a $9.50 strike price call, then you maintain your stock position as long as the stock price stays below $9.50 at expiration. If the stock price moves to $10, you only profit up to $9.50, so your profit is $9.50 - $9.00 + $0.10 = $0.60.

If you sell an ITM call option, the underlying stock's price will need to fall below the call's strike price for you to maintain your shares. If this occurs, you will likely be facing a loss on your stock position, but you will still own your shares, and you will have received the premium to help offset the loss.

Strategies Of Covered calls

Selling the call obligates you to sell stock you already own at strike price A if the option is assigned. Some investors will run this strategy after they've already seen nice gains on the stock. Often, they will sell out-of-the-money calls, so if the stock price goes up, they're willing to part with the stock and take the profit.

Covered calls can also be used to achieve income on the stock above and beyond any dividends. The goal in that case is for the options to expire worthless. If you buy the stock and sell the calls all at the same time, it's called a "Buy / Write." Some investors use a Buy / Write as a way to lower the cost basis of a stock they've just purchased.

Strategies

Current stock price minus the premium received for selling the call.

1. The sweet spot for this strategy depends on your objective. If you are selling covered calls to earn income on your stock, then you want the stock to remain as close to the strike price as possible without going above it.

2. If you want to sell the stock while making additional profit by selling the calls, then you want the stock to rise above the strike price and stay there at expiration. That way, the calls will be assigned.

3. However, you probably don't want the stock to shoot too high, or you might be a bit disappointed that you parted with it. But don't fret if that happens. You still made out all right on the stock. Do yourself a favor and stop getting quotes on it.

4. When the call is first sold, potential profit is limited to the strike price minus the current stock price plus the premium received for selling the call.

5. You receive a premium for selling the option, but most downside risk comes from owning the stock, which may potentially lose its value. However, selling the option does create an "opportunity risk." That is, if the stock price skyrockets, the calls might be assigned and you'll miss out on those gains.

Because You Own The Stock, No Additional Margin Is Required.

For this strategy, time decay is your friend. You want the price of the option you sold to approach zero. That means if you choose to close your position before expiration, it will be less expensive to buy it back. After the strategy is established, you want implied volatility to decrease. That will decrease the price of the option you sold, so if you choose to close your position before expiration it will be less expensive to do so.

Covered Call Example

An investor owns shares of hypothetical company TSJ. They like its long-term prospects as well as its share price but feel in the shorter term the stock will likely trade relatively flat, perhaps within a couple dollars of its current price of $25. If they sell a call option on TSJ with a strike price of $27, they earn the premium from the option sale but, for the duration of the option, cap their upside on the stock to $27. Assume the premium they receive for writing a three-month call option is $0.75 ($75 per contract or 100 shares).

One Of Two Scenarios Will Play Out:

1. TSJ shares trade below the $27 strike price. The option will expire worthless and the investor will keep the premium from the option. In this case, by using the buy-write strategy they have successfully outperformed the stock. They still own the stock but have an extra $75 in their pocket, less fees.

2. TSJ shares rise above $27. The option is exercised, and the upside in the stock is capped at $27. If price goes above $27.75 (strike price plus premium), the investor would have been better off holding the stock. Although, if they planned to sell at $27 anyway, writing the call option gave them an extra $0.75 per share.

Chapter 6 - Buying Calls

Call Option

Definition: A call option is an option contract in which the holder (buyer) has the right (but not the obligation) to buy a specified quantity of a security at a specified price (strike price) within a fixed period (until its expiration).

For the writer (seller) of a call option, it represents an obligation to sell the underlying security at the strike price if the option is exercised. The call option writer is paid a premium for taking on the risk associated with the obligation.

What Is A Call Option?

A call option, commonly referred to as a "call," is a form of a derivatives contract that gives the call option buyer the right, but not the obligation, to buy a stock or other financial instrument at a specific price – the strike price of the option – within a specified time frame. The seller of the option is obligated to sell the security to the buyer if the latter decides to exercise their option to make a purchase. The buyer of the option can exercise the option at any time before a specified expiration date. The expiration date may be three months, six months, or even one year in the future. The seller receives the purchase price for the option, which is based on how close the option strike price is to the price of the underlying security at the time the option is purchased, and on how long a period remains till the option's expiration date. In other words, the price of the option is based on how likely, or unlikely, it is that the option buyer will have a chance to profitably exercise the option before expiration. Usually, options are sold in lots of 100 shares.

The buyer of a call option seeks to make a profit if and when the price of the underlying asset increases to a price higher than the option strike price. On the other hand, the seller of the call option hopes that the price of the asset will decline, or at least never rise as high as the option strike/exercise price before it expires, in which case the money received for selling the option will be pure profit. If the price of the underlying security does not increase beyond the strike price before expiration, then it will not be profitable for the option buyer to exercise the option, and the option will expire worthless or "out-of-the-money". The buyer will suffer a loss equal to the price paid for the call option. Alternatively, if the price of the underlying security rises above the option strike price, the buyer can profitably exercise the option.

For example, assume you bought an option on 100 shares of a stock, with an option strike price of $30. Before your option expires, the price of the stock rises from $28 to $40. Then you could exercise your right to buy 100 shares of the stock at $30, immediately giving you a $10 per share profit. Your net profit would be 100 shares, times $10 a share, minus whatever purchase price you paid for the option. In this example, if you had paid $200 for the call option, then your net profit would be $800 (100 shares x $10 per share – $200 = $800).

Buying call options enables investors to invest a small amount of capital to potentially profit from a price rise in the underlying security, or to hedge away from positional risks. Small investors use options to try to turn small amounts of money into big profits, while corporate and institutional investors use options to increase their marginal revenues and hedge their stock portfolios.

How Do Call Options Work?

Since call options are derivative instruments, their prices are derived from the price of an underlying security, such as a stock. For example, if a buyer purchases the call option of ABC at a strike price of $100 and with an expiration date of December 31, they will have the right to buy 100 shares of the company any time before or on December 31. The buyer can also sell the options contract to another option buyer at any time before the expiration date, at the prevailing market price of the contract. If the price of the underlying security remains relatively unchanged or declines, then the value of the option will decline as it nears its expiration date.

Investors Use Call Options For The Following Purposes:

1. Speculation

Call options allow their holders to potentially gain profits from a price rise in an underlying stock while paying only a fraction of the cost of buying actual stock shares. They are a leveraged investment that offers potentially unlimited profits and limited losses (the price paid for the option). Due to the high degree of leverage, call options are considered high-risk investments.

2. Hedging

Investment banks and other institutions use call options as hedging instruments. Just like insurance, hedging with an option opposite your position helps to limit the amount of losses on the underlying instrument should an unforeseen event occur. Call options can be bought and used to hedge short stock portfolios, or sold to hedge against a pullback in long stock portfolios.

Call options are a type of option that increases in value when a stock rises. They're the best-known kind of option, and they allow the owner to lock in a price to buy a specific stock by a specific date. Call options are appealing because they can appreciate quickly on a small move up in the stock price. So that makes them a favorite with traders who are looking for a big gain.

How Does A Call Option Work?

A call option gives you the right, but not the requirement, to purchase a stock at a specific price (known as the strike price) by a specific date, at the option's expiration. For this right, the call buyer will pay an amount of money called a premium, which the call seller will receive. Unlike stocks, which can live in perpetuity, an option will cease to exist after expiration, ending up either worthless or with some value. The following components comprise the major traits of an option:

❖ **Strike price:** The price at which you can buy the underlying stock

❖ **Premium:** The price of the option, for either buyer or seller

❖ **Expiration:** When the option expires and is settled

One option is called a contract, and each contract represents 100 shares of the underlying stock. Exchanges quote options prices in terms of the per-share price, not the total price you must pay to own the contract. For example, an option may be quoted at $0.75 on the exchange. So to purchase one contract it will cost (100 shares * 1 contract * $0.75), or $75.

Call options are in the money when the stock price is above the strike price at expiration. The call owner can exercise the option, putting up cash to buy the stock at the strike price. Or the owner can simply sell the option at its fair market value to another buyer.

A call owner profits when the premium paid is less than the difference between the stock price and the strike price. For example, imagine a trader bought a call for $0.50 with a strike price of $20, and the stock is $23. The option is worth $3 and the trader has made a profit of $2.50.

If the stock price is below the strike price at expiration, then the call is out of the money and expires worthless. The call seller keeps any premium received for the option.

Why Buy A Call Option?

The biggest advantage of buying a call option is that it magnifies the gains in a stock's price. For a relatively small upfront cost, you can enjoy a stock's gains above the strike price until the option expires. So if you're buying a call, you usually expect the stock to rise before expiration. Imagine that a stock named XYZ is trading at $20 per share. You can buy a call on the stock with a $20 strike price for $2 with an expiration in eight months. One contract costs $200, or $2 * * 1 contract * 100 shares.

Why Sell A Call Option?

For every call bought, there is a call sold. So what are the advantages of selling a call? In short, the payoff structure is exactly the reverse for buying a call. Call sellers expect the stock to remain flat or decline, and hope to pocket the premium without any consequences. Let's use the same example as before. Imagine that stock XYZ is trading at $20 per share. You can sell a call on the stock with a $20 strike price for $2 with an expiration in eight months. One contract gives you $200, or ($2 * 100 shares).

Buying Call Options

Call buying is the simplest way of trading call options. Novice traders often start trading options by buying calls, not only because of its simplicity but also due to the large ROI generated from successful trades.

The buyer of a call option is referred to as a holder. The holder purchases a call option with the hope that the price will rise beyond the strike price and before the expiration date. The profit earned equals the sale proceeds, minus strike price, premium, and any transactional fees associated with the sale. If the price does not increase beyond the strike price, the buyer will not exercise the option. The buyer will suffer a loss equal to the premium of the call option. For example, suppose ABC Company's stock is selling at $40 and a call option contract with a strike price of $40 and an expiry of one month is priced at $2. The buyer is optimistic that the stock price will rise and pays $200 for one ABC call option with a strike price of $40. If the stock of ABC increases from $40 to $50, the buyer will receive a gross profit of $1000 and a net profit of $800.

Selling Call Options

Instead of purchasing call options, one can also sell (write) them for a profit. Call option writers, also known as sellers, sell call options with the hope that they expire worthless so that they can pocket the premiums. Selling calls, or short call, involves more risk but can also be very profitable when done properly. One can sell covered calls or naked (uncovered) calls.

Call option sellers, also known as writers, sell call options with the hope that they become worthless at the expiry date. They make money by pocketing the premiums (price) paid to them. Their profit will be reduced, or may even result in a net loss if the option buyer exercises their option profitably when the underlying security price rises above the option strike price. Call options are sold in the following two ways:

1. Covered Call Option

A call option is covered if the seller of the call option owns the underlying stock. Selling the call options on these underlying stocks results in additional income, and will offset any expected declines in the stock price. The option seller is "covered" against a loss since if the option buyer exercises their option, the seller can provide the buyer with shares of the stock that he has already purchased at a price below the strike price of the option. The seller's profit in owning the underlying stock will be limited to the stock's rise to the option strike price but he will be protected against any actual loss.

2. Naked Call Option

A naked call option is when an option seller sells a call option without owning the underlying stock. Naked short selling of options is considered very risky since there is no limit to how high a stock's price can go and the option seller is not "covered" against potential losses by owning the underlying stock. When a call option buyer exercises his right, the naked option seller is obligated to buy the stock at the current market price to provide the shares to the option holder. If the stock price exceeds the call option's strike price, then the difference between the current market price and the strike price represents the loss to the seller. Most option sellers charge a high fee to compensate for any losses that may occur.

Call vs. Put Option

A call and put option are the opposite of each other. A call option is the right to buy an underlying stock at a predetermined price up until a specified expiration date. On the contrary, a put option is the right to sell the underlying stock at a predetermined price until a fixed expiry date. While a call option buyer has the right (but not obligation) to buy shares at the strike price before or on the expiry date, a put option buyer has the right to sell shares at the strike price.

Call Spreads

A call spread is an options strategy in which equal number of call option contracts are bought and sold simultaneously on the same underlying security but with different strike prices and/or expiration dates. Call spreads limit the option trader's maximum loss at the expense of capping his potential profit at the same time.

Buying A Call Option

Traders buy a call option in the commodities or futures markets if they expect the underlying futures price to move higher. Buying a call option entitles the buyer of the option the right to purchase the underlying futures contract at the strike price any time before the contract expires. This rarely happens, and there is not much benefit to doing this, so don't get caught up in the formal definition of buying a call option.

Most traders buy call options because they believe a commodity market is going to move higher and they want to profit from that move. You can also exit the option before it expires during market hours, of course. All options have a limited life. They are defined by a specific expiration date by the futures exchange where it trades. You can visit each futures exchange's website for specific expiration dates of each commodities market.

Finding The Proper Call Options To Buy

You must first decide on your objectives and then find the best option to buy. Things to consider when buying call options include:

- ❖ Duration of time you plan on being in the trade
- ❖ The amount you can allocate to buying a call option
- ❖ The length of a move you expect from the market

Most commodities and futures have a wide range of options in different expiration months and different strike prices that allow you to pick an option that meets your objectives.

Duration Of Time You Plan On Being In The Call Option Trade

This will help you determine how much time you need for a call option. If you are expecting a commodity to complete its move higher within two weeks, you will want to buy a commodity with at least two weeks remaining on it. Typically, you don't want to buy an option with six to nine months remaining if you only plan on being in the trade for a couple of weeks, since the options will be more expensive and you will lose some leverage.

One thing to be aware of is that the time premium of options decays more rapidly in the last 30 days.[1] Therefore, you could be correct in your assumptions about a trade, but the option loses too much time value and you end up with a loss. We suggest that you always buy an option with 30 more days than you expect to be in the trade.

Amount You Can Allocate To Buying A Call Option

Depending on your account size and risk tolerances, some options may be too expensive for you to buy, or they might not be the right options altogether. In the money call, options will be more expensive than out of the money options. Also, the more time remaining on the call options there is, the more they will cost. Unlike futures contracts, there is a margin when you buy most options. You have to pay the whole option premium up front. Therefore, options in volatile markets like crude oil can cost several thousand dollars. That may not be suitable for all options traders, and you don't want to make the mistake of buying deep out of the money options just because they are in your price range. Most deep out of the money options will expire worthlessly, and they are considered long shots.

Length Of A Move You Expect From The Market

To maximize your leverage and control your risk, you should have an idea of what type of move you expect from the commodity or futures market. The more conservative approach is usually to buy in the money options. A more aggressive approach is to buy multiple contracts of out of the money options. Your returns will increase with multiple contracts of out-of-the-money options if the market makes a large move higher. It is also riskier as you have a greater chance of losing the entire option premium if the market doesn't move.

Call Options Vs. A Futures Contract

Your losses on buying a call option are limited to the premium you paid for the option plus commissions and any fees. With a futures contract, you have virtually unlimited loss potential. Call options also do not move as quickly as futures contracts unless they are deep in the money. This allows a commodity trader to ride out many of the ups and downs in the markets that might force a trader to close a futures contract to limit risk. One of the major drawbacks to buying options is the fact that options lose time value every day. Options are a wasting asset. You not only have to be correct regarding the direction of the market but also on the timing of the move.

Break Even Point On Buying Call Options

Strike Price + Option Premium Paid

This formula is used at option expiration considering there is no time value left on the call options. You can sell the options anytime before expiration and there will be time premium remaining unless the options are deep in the money or far out of the money.

A Stop-Loss Instrument

A call option can also serve as a limited-risk stop-loss instrument for a short position. In volatile markets, traders and investors should use stops against risk positions. A stop is a function of risk-reward, and as the most successful market participants know, you should never risk more than you are looking to make on any investment.

Facts: The problem with stops is that sometimes the market can trade to a level that triggers a stop and then reverse. For those with short positions, a long call option serves as stop-loss protection, but it can give you more time than a stop that closes the position when it trades to the risk level. That is because if the option has time left if the market becomes volatile, the call option serves two purposes.

1. First, the call option will act as price insurance, protecting the short position from additional losses above the strike price.

2. Second, and perhaps more importantly, the call option allows the opportunity to stay short even if the price moves above the insured level or the strike price.

Markets often rise only to turn around and fall dramatically after the price triggers stop orders. As long as the option still has time until expiration, the call option will keep a market participant in a short position and allow them to survive a volatile period that eventually returns to a downtrend. A short position together with a long call is essentially the same as a long put position, which has limited risk. Call options are instruments that can be employed to position directly in a market to bet that the price will appreciate or to protect an existing short position from an adverse price move.

Covered Calls For Income

Some investors use call options to generate income through a covered call strategy. This strategy involves owning an underlying stock while at the same time writing a call option, or giving someone else the right to buy your stock. The investor collects the option premium and hopes the option expires worthless (below strike price). This strategy generates additional income for the investor but can also limit profit potential if the underlying stock price rises sharply.

Covered calls work because if the stock rises above the strike price, the option buyer will exercise their right to buy the stock at the lower strike price. This means the option writer doesn't profit on the stock's movement above the strike price. The options writer's maximum profit on the option is the premium received.

Using Options For Speculation

Options contracts allow buyers to obtain significant exposure to a stock for a relatively small price. Used in isolation, they can provide significant gains if a stock rises. But they can also result in a 100% loss of premium, if the call option expires worthless due to the underlying stock price failing to move above the strike price. The benefit of buying call options is that risk is always capped at the premium paid for the option.

Investors may also buy and sell different call options simultaneously, creating a call spread. These will cap both the potential profit and loss from the strategy, but are more cost-effective in some cases than a single call option since the premium collected from one option's sale offsets the premium paid for the other.

Using Options For Tax Management

Investors sometimes use options to change portfolio allocations without actually buying or selling the underlying security.

For example, an investor may own 100 shares of XYZ stock and may be liable for a large unrealized capital gain. Not wanting to trigger a taxable event, shareholders may use options to reduce the exposure to the underlying security without actually selling it. While gains from call and put options are also taxable, their treatment by the IRS is more complex because of the multiple types and varieties of options. In the case above, the only cost to the shareholder for engaging in this strategy is the cost of the options contract itself.

Real World Example Of A Call Option

Suppose that Microsoft shares are trading at $108 per share. You own 100 shares of the stock and want to generate an income above and beyond the stock's dividend. You also believe that shares are unlikely to rise above $115.00 per share over the next month.

You take a look at the call options for the following month and see that there's a 115.00 call trading at $0.37 per contract. So, you sell one call option and collect the $37 premium ($0.37 x 100 shares), representing a roughly four percent annualized income.

If the stock rises above $115.00, the option buyer will exercise the option and you will have to deliver the 100 shares of stock at $115.00 per share. You still generated a profit of $7.00 per share, but you will have missed out on any upside above $115.00. If the stock doesn't rise above $115.00, you keep the shares and the $37 in premium income.

Chapter 7 - Volatility in The Markets

Options prices depend crucially on estimated future volatility of the underlying asset. As a result, while all the other inputs to an option's price are known, people will have varying expectations of volatility. Trading volatility therefore becomes a key set of strategies used by options traders.

There are seven factors or variables that determine the price of an option. Of these seven variables, six have known values, and there is no ambiguity about their input values into an option pricing model. But the seventh variable volatility is only an estimate, and for this reason, it is the most important factor in determining the price of an option.

- ❖ The current price of the underlying - known
- ❖ Strike price - known
- ❖ Type of option (Call or Put) - known
- ❖ Time to the expiration of the option - known
- ❖ Risk-free interest rate - known
- ❖ Dividends on the underlying - known
- ❖ Volatility - unknown

Volatile Options Trading Strategies

Options trading has two big advantages over almost every other form of trading. One is the ability to generate profits when you predict a financial instrument will be relatively stable in price, and the second is the ability to make money when you believe that a financial instrument is volatile.

When a stock or another security is volatile it means that a large price swing is likely, but it's difficult to predict in which direction. By using volatile options trading strategies, it's possible to make trades where you will profit providing an underlying security moves significantly in price, regardless of which direction it moves in.

Many scenarios can lead to a financial instrument being volatile. For example, a company may be about to release its financial reports or announce some other big news, either of which probably lead to its stock being volatile. Rumors of an impending takeover could have the same effect. What this means is that there are usually plenty of opportunities to make profits through using volatile options trading strategies. On this page, we look at the concept of such strategies in more detail and provide a comprehensive list of strategies in this category.

What Are Volatile Options Trading Strategies?

Quite simply, volatile options trading strategies are designed specifically to make profits from stocks or other securities that are likely to experience a dramatic price movement, without having to predict in which direction that price movement will be. Given that making a judgment about which direction the price of a volatile security will move in is very difficult, it's clear why such they can be useful.

There are also known as dual directional strategies, because they can make profits from price movements in either direction. The basic principle of using them is that you combine multiple positions that have unlimited potential profits but limited losses so that you will make a profit providing the underlying security moves far in enough in one direction or the other. The simplest example of this in practice is the long straddle, which combines buying an equal amount of call options and put options on the same underlying security with the same strike price.

Buying call options (a long call) has limited losses, the amount you spend on them, but unlimited potential gains as you can make as much as price of the underlying security goes up by.

Buying put options (a long put) also has limited losses and almost unlimited gains. The potential gains are limited only by the amount which the price of the underlying security can fall by (i.e. its full value).

By combining these two positions into one overall position, you should make a return whichever direction the underlying security moves in. The idea is that if the underlying security goes up, you make more profit from the long call than you lose from the long put. If the underlying security goes down, then you make more profit from the long put than you lose from the long call.

Of course, this isn't without its risks. If the price of the underlying security goes up, but not by enough to make the long call profits greater than the long put losses, then you'll lose money. Equally, if the price of the underlying security goes down, but not by enough so the long put profits are greater than the long call losses, then you will also lose money.

Small price moves aren't enough to make profits from this, or any other, volatile strategy. To reiterate, strategies of this type should only be used when you are expecting an underlying security to move significantly in price.

List Of Volatile Options Trading Strategies

Below is a list of the volatile options trading strategies that are most commonly used by options traders. We have included some very basic information about each one here, but you can get more details by clicking on the relevant link. If you require some extra assistance in choosing which one to use and when, you may find our Selection Tool useful. Options strategies for a volatile market are the ones that enable traders to sail over and profit from wild price swings in the market in any direction that is, whether the prices rise, fall or stay neutral. Here the real challenge is to gauge how much the surge would be, to make the best options strategy decisions. Here are some of the best options strategies for volatile market. These are important and yet simple ones from which even beginners to stock investing can benefit.

Long Straddle: We have briefly discussed the long straddle above. It's one of the simplest volatile strategies and perfectly suitable for beginners. Two transactions are involved and it creates a debit spread.

Long Strangle: This is a very similar strategy to the long straddle, but has a lower upfront cost. It's also suitable for beginners.

Strip Straddle: This is best used when your outlook is volatile but you think a fall in price is the most likely. It's simple, involves two transactions to create a debit spread, and is suitable for beginners.

Strip Strangle: This is a cheaper alternative to the strip straddle. It also involves two transactions and is well suited for beginners.

Strap Straddle: You would use this when your outlook is volatile but you believe that a rise in price is the most likely. It is another simple strategy that is suitable for beginners.

Strap Strangle: The strap strangle is essentially a lower cost alternative to the strap saddle. This simple strategy involves two transactions and is suitable for beginners.

Long Gut: This is a simple, but relatively expensive, strategy that is suitable for beginners. Two transactions are involved to create a debit spread.

Call Ratio Backspread: This more complicated strategy is suitable for when your outlook is volatile but you think a price rise is more likely than a price fall. Two transactions are used to create a credit spread and it is not recommended for beginners.

Put Ratio Backspread: This is a slightly complex strategy that you would use if your outlook is volatile but you favour a price fall over a price rise. A credit spread is created using two transactions and it is not suitable for beginners.

Short Calendar Call Spread: This is an advanced strategy that involves two transactions. It creates a credit spread and is not recommended for beginners.

Short Calendar Put Spread: This is an advanced strategy that is not suitable for beginners. It involves two transactions and creates a credit spread.

Short Butterfly Spread: This complex strategy involves three transactions and creates a credit spread. It isn't suitable for beginners.

Short Condor Spread: This advanced strategy involves four transactions. A credit spread is created and it isn't suitable for beginners.

Short Albatross Spread: This is a complex trading strategy that involves four transactions to create a credit spread. It isn't recommended for beginners.

Reverse Iron Butterfly Spread: There are four transactions involved in this, which create a debit spread. It's complex and not recommended for beginners.

Reverse Iron Condor Spread: This advanced strategy creates a debit spread and involves four transactions. It isn't suitable for beginners.

Reverse Iron Albatross Spread: This is a complex trading strategy that is not suitable for beginners. It creates a debit spread using four transactions.

Trading options is more than just being bullish or bearish or market neutral. There's volatility. Limitations on capital. Stronger or weaker directional biases. Whatever the scenario, you have the choice of a logical option strategy that can be risk-defined, capital-effective, and/or have a higher probability of profit than simply buying or shorting stock. By sorting each strategy into buckets covering each potential combination of these three variables, you can create a handy reference guide. You could even print it out and tape it to your wall. Doing so might help you run through the process of making speedy trading decisions should you need or if warranted.

We'll help you get started with this list of strategies designed for a high-volatility market environment. Notice how most of them are composed of the basic vertical and calendar spreads. As you review them, keep in mind that there are no guarantees with these strategies.

Volatility vs. Risk

It's important to understand the difference between volatility and risk before deciding on a trading method. Volatility in the financial markets is seen as extreme and rapid price swings. Risk is the possibility of losing some or all of an investment. As volatility of the market increases, so do profit potential and the risk of loss. There's usually a marked increase in the frequency of trades during these periods and a corresponding decrease in the amount of time that positions are held. Also, a hypersensitivity to news is often reflected in market prices during times of extreme volatility.

Probability-Based Investing

Although investors' consensus will usually result in a relatively efficient stock price that reflects all known information, there are times when one or more key pieces of data about a company are not widely disseminated. That can result in an inefficient stock price that's not reflected in its beta. The investor is, therefore, taking an additional risk of which he or she is most likely unaware. Probability-based investing is one strategy that can be used to help determine whether this factor applies to a given stock or security. Investors who use this strategy will compare the company's future growth as anticipated by the market with the company's actual financial data, including current cash flow and historical growth. This comparison helps calculate the probability that the stock price is truly reflecting all pertinent data. Companies that stand up to the criteria of this analysis are therefore considered more likely to achieve the future growth level that the market perceives them to possess.

Directional vs. Non-Directional Investing

Most private investors practice directional investing, which requires the markets to move consistently in a desired direction (it can be either up or down). Market timers, long or short equity investors, and trend investors all rely on directional investing strategies. Times of increased volatility can result in a directionless or sideways market, repeatedly triggering stop losses. Gains earned over years can be eroded in a few days. Non-directional investors attempt to take advantage of market inefficiencies and relative pricing discrepancies. Next, we'll take a look at some of those strategies.

Equity-Market-Neutral Strategy

Here is where stock pickers can shine because the ability to pick the right stock is just about all that matters with this strategy. The goal is to leverage differences in stock prices by being both long and short among stocks in the same sector, industry, nation, market cap, etc.

By focusing on the sector and not the market as a whole, you emphasize movement within a category. Consequently, a loss on a short position can be quickly offset by a gain on a long one. The trick is to identify the standout and the underperforming stocks. The principle behind the equity-market-neutral strategy is that your gains will be more closely linked to the difference between the best and worst performers than the overall market performance and less susceptible to market volatility.

Merger Arbitrage

Many private investors have noticed that the stocks of two companies involved in a potential merger or acquisition often react differently to the news of the impending action and try to take advantage of the shareholders' reaction. Often the acquirer's stock is discounted while the stock of the company to be acquired rises in anticipation of the buyout. A merger arbitrage strategy attempts to take advantage of the fact that the stocks combined generally trade at a discount to the post-merger price due to the risk that any merger could fall apart. Hoping that the merger will close, the investor simultaneously buys the target company's stock and shorts the acquiring company's stock.

Relative Value Arbitrage

The relative value approach seeks out a correlation between securities and is typically used during a sideways market. What kinds of pairs are ideal? They are heavyweight stocks within the same industry that share a significant amount of trading history. Once you've identified the similarities, it's time to wait for their paths to diverge. A divergence of 5% or larger lasting two days or more signals that you can open a position in both securities with the expectation they will eventually converge. You can long the undervalued security and short the overvalued one, and then close both positions once they converge.

Event-Driven Strategy

This scenario is triggered by corporate upheaval, whether it be a merger, asset sale, restructuring, or even bankruptcy. Any of these events can temporarily inflate or deflate a company's stock price while the market attempts to judge and value these newest developments. This strategy does require analytical skills to identify the core issue and what will resolve it, as well as the ability to determine individual performance relative to the market in general.

Trading On Volatility

Investors who seek profits from market volatility can trade ETFs or ETNs that track a volatility index. One such index is the Volatility Index (VIX) created by the Chicago Board Options Exchange (CBOE). Volatile times provide an opportunity to reconsider your investment strategy. Although the approaches described here are not for all investors, they can be leveraged by experienced traders. Alternatively, each option is available through a professional money manager.

Chapter 8 - Buying and Selling Puts of an Option Trading

Options are financial contracts to buy or sell a particular stock at a set price for a specified period. A call option, which gives the owner the right to buy stock, is the most common type of option, but it's not the only type. You can also trade put options, which give the owner the right to sell stock. How you use a put option depends on what you want to accomplis In options terminology, "writing" is the same as selling an option, and "naked" refers to strategies in which the underlying security is not owned and options are written against this phantom security position. The naked strategy is aggressive and higher risk but can be used to generate income as part of a diversified portfolio. However, if not used properly, a naked call position can have disastrous consequences since a security can theoretically rise to infinity.

To understand why an investor would choose to sell an option, you must first understand what type of option it is that he or she is selling, and what kind of payoff he or she is expecting to make when the price of the underlying asset moves in the desired direction.

Long Put

If you expect the market price of a particular stock to decline in the near term, you might employ a long put option, which involves buying a put. Owning the put gives you the right, but not the obligation, to sell 100 shares of the underlying stock for a set price, called the strike price, until the option reaches its expiration date, at which time the option expires, becomes worthless and ceases to exist. If the stock's market price declines below the strike price, the value of your put option will rise. You don't have to own the underlying stock. You can instead sell your put option for its market price and pocket the profit. If the stock price does not decline below the strike price, the worst you can do is lose the premium you paid for the put option.

Protective Put

If you own a stock you think is vulnerable to a downturn in the market, but you believe the stock also has some good upside potential, you might consider employing a protective put strategy. This involves buying a put option on the same stock you own, but at a strike price that is below the stock's current market price. If the stock price rises, you get a nice gain on the stock, but your put option will expire and become worthless, so you'll lose the amount of the premium you paid for it. If the stock price plummets, you can exercise your put option and sell your stock for the strike price, limiting your loss on the stock to a predetermined level.

Cash-Secured Put

You can generate a steady stream of income by selling, also known as writing, cash-secured put options. This strategy involves selling put options with a strike price that is at or below the stock's current market price. You'll receive a premium for agreeing to buy the stock for the strike price if the put option is exercised. If the stock's market price increases, the option will expire, you get to keep the premium and you can sell another put option and collect another premium. If the stock price declines and the option is exercised, you have enough cash set aside in your brokerage account to cover the purchase price, which will be offset somewhat by the premium you received for selling the put.

Bear Put Spread

A bear put spread is a conservative option strategy that involves buying a put option while at the same time writing another put option on the same stock with the same expiration date but with a lower strike price. If the stock price declines below the long put strike price, the options value increases and you make a profit. You also have a profit from the premium you received from selling the put. The trade-off happens if the stock price continues to decline below the strike price for your short put, in which case the option could be exercised, requiring you to buy the stock.

How To Sell Put Options To Benefit In Any Market

Selling (writing) a put option allows an investor to potentially own the underlying security at a future date and a much more favorable price. In other words, the sale of put options allows market players to gain bullish exposure, with the added benefit of potentially owning the underlying security at a future date and a price below the current market price.

Call Options vs. Put Options

A quick primer on options may help understand how writing (selling) puts can benefit your investment strategy, so let's examine a typical trading scenario as well as potential risks and rewards.

An equity option is a derivative instrument that acquires its value from the underlying security. Buying a call option gives the holder the right to own the security at a predetermined price, known as the option exercise price. Conversely, a put option gives the owner the right to sell the underlying security at the option exercise price. Thus, buying a call option is a bullish bet the owner makes money when the security goes up while a put option is a bearish bet - the owner makes money when the security goes down.

Selling a call or put option flips over this directional logic. More importantly, the writer takes on an obligation to the counterparty when selling an option because it carries a commitment to honor the position if the buyer of the option decides to exercise their right to own the security outright.

Here's a summary breakdown of buying vs. selling options.

Buying A Call: You have the right to buy a security at a predetermined price.

Selling A Call: You must deliver the security at a predetermined price to the option buyer if they exercise the option.

Buying A Put: You have the right to sell a security at a predetermined price.

Selling A Put: You must buy the security at a predetermined price from the option buyer if they exercise the option.

Characteristics Of Prudent Put Selling

Sell puts only if you're comfortable owning the underlying security at the predetermined price, because you're assuming an obligation to buy if the counterparty chooses to exercise the option. Only enter trades where the net price paid for the underlying security is attractive. This is the most important consideration in selling puts profitably in any market environment.

Other benefits of put selling can be exploited once this important pricing rule is satisfied. The ability to generate portfolio income sits at thea top of this list because the seller keeps the entire premium if the sold put expires without exercise by the counterparty. Another key benefit is the opportunity to own the underlying security at a price below the current market price.

Put Selling In Practice

Let's look at an example of prudent put selling. Shares in Company A are dazzling investors with increasing profits from its revolutionary products. The stock is currently trading at $270 and the price-to-earnings ratio is at a level that is an extremely reasonable valuation for this company's fast growth track. If you're bullish about their prospects, you can buy 100 shares for $27,000 plus commissions and fees.

As an alternative, you could sell one January $250 put option expiring two years from now for just $30. That means the option will expire on the third Friday of January two years from now and has an exercise price of $250. One option contract covers 100 shares, allowing you to collect $3,000 in options premium over time, less commission.

By selling this option, you're agreeing to buy 100 shares of Company A for $250 no later than January two years from now. Since Company A shares are trading for $270 today, the put buyer isn't going to ask you to buy the shares for $250. So, you'll collect the premium while you wait.

If the stock drops to $250 in January two years from now, you'll be required to buy the 100 shares at that price, but you'll keep the premium of $30 per share so your net cost will be $220 per share. If shares never fall to $250, the option will expire worthless and you'll keep the entire $3,000 premium.

Summing up, as an alternative to buying 100 shares for $27,000, you can sell the put and lower your net cost to $220 a share (or $22,000 if the price falls to $250 per share). If the option expires worthless, you get to keep the $30 per share premium, which represents a 12 percent return on a $250 buy price.

You can see why it's attractive to sell puts on securities you want to own. If Company A declines, you'll be required to cough up $25,000 to buy the shares at $250 (having kept the $3,000 premium, your net cost will be $22,000). Keep in mind your broker can force you to sell other holdings to buy this position if you don't have available cash in your account.

Chapter 9 - Options Trading Jargon

Options Trading Glossary Of Terms

The fundamentals of options trading are relatively easy to learn, but this is a very complex subject once you get into the more advanced aspects. As such it's no surprise that there is a fair amount of terminology and jargon involved that you may not be familiar with. We have compiled this comprehensive glossary of terms to be a useful reference tool for anyone learning about trading options.

Although we always try and explain any terminology we use in the context that we are using it in any particular page or article we write, there may be occasions when you come across a term that you don't understand. This glossary of terms is here to be used if you ever require an explanation for what a particular word or phrase means.

A

Albatross Spread: This is an advanced strategy that can be used to profit from an underlying security remaining neutral. Learn how to use an Albatross Spread.

All Or None Order: Often abbreviated as AON, this is a type of order that must be either filled entirely or not at all.

American Style Option: A contract that gives the holder the flexibility of choosing to exercise their option at any point between buying the contract and the contract expiring. More on American Style.

Approval Levels: See Trading Levels.

Arbitrage: Taking advantage of price discrepancies by buying and selling to create a risk free trade.

Arbitrage Trading Strategies: Strategies that involve the use of arbitrage. Read more at Arbitrage Strategies.

Ask Price: The price it costs to buy an option.

Assignment: When the writer of a contract is required to fulfill their obligations under the terms of that contract – for example buying the underlying security if they have written calls or selling the underlying security if they have written puts. The writer will be issued with an assignment notice in such circumstances.

At The Money Option: An option where the price of the underlying security is the same as the strike price.

Automatic Exercise: The process by which in the money options are automatically exercised if they are in the money at the point of expiration.

Auto Trading: A trading method that involves using a third party to select your trades and having your broker automatically execute them. Read more on Auto Trading.

B

Basket Option: A type of option that is based on a group of underlying securities rather than just one.

Barrier Option: A type of option that can come into existence or go out of existence based on specific criteria is usually related to the price of the underlying security. More about Barrier Options.

Bear Butterfly Spread: This is an advanced strategy that can be used when the outlook of an underlying security is bearish. Learn how to use a Bear Butterfly Spread.

Bear Call Spread: A simple strategy, using calls, that can be used when the expectation is that the underlying security will decline in price. Learn how to use a Bear Call Spread.

Bearish: An expectation that an option, or any financial instrument, will decrease in price.

Bearish Trading Strategies: Strategies that can be used to profit from a downward move in the price of a financial instrument. List of Bearish Strategies.

Bear Market: When the overall market is in decline.

Bear Put Ladder Spread: This is an advanced strategy that can be used when the outlook on an underlying security is bearish. Learn how to use a Bear Put Ladder Spread.

Bear Put Spread: A simple strategy using puts that can be used when the expectation is that the underlying security will decline in price. Learn how to use a Bear Put Spread.

Bear Ratio Spread: This is a strategy that can be used when the outlook on an underlying security is bearish. Learn how to use a Bear Ratio Spread.

Bear Spread: A spread that is created to profit from bearish movements.

Bear Trap: An unconfirmed market movement which suggests a bear market, but is unconfirmed and ends up with the market moving upwards.

Bid Price: The price at which an option can be sold.

Bid Ask Spread: The difference between the bid price and the ask price of an option. An indicator of liquidity, and often referred to simply as the spread.

Binary Option: A type of option that pays a fixed return if it expires in the money or nothing if it expires at the money or out of the money. More about Binary Options.

Binomial Options Pricing Model: Can be abbreviated to BOPM; a pricing model that was developed by Cox, Ross and Rubinstein in 1979. Read more about the Binomial Pricing Model.

Black Scholes Options Pricing Model: A pricing model that is based on factors that include the strike price, the price of the underlying security, the length of time until expiration, and volatility. Read about the Black Scholes Pricing Model.

Box Spread: An advanced strategy that involves the use of arbitrage.

Break Even Point: The price or price range of the underlying security at which a strategy will break even, with no profits and no losses.

Breakout: When the price of a security moves above an existing resistance level or below an existing support level. The expectation is that the security will continue to move in the prevailing direction.

Broker: An individual or a company that executes orders to buy and sell financial instruments on behalf of clients.

Broker Commissions: The charge from a broker for executing orders on behalf of clients.

Bull Butterfly Spread: This is a strategy that can be used when the outlook on an underlying security is bullish. Learn how to use a Bull Butterfly Spread.

Bull Call Ladder Spread: This is a strategy that can be used when the outlook on an underlying security is bullish. Learn how to use a Bull Call Ladder Spread.

Bull Call Spread: A simple strategy, involving calls, which can be used when the expectation is that the underlying security will increase in price. Learn how to use a Bull Call Spread.

Bull Condor Spread: This is an advanced strategy that can be used when the outlook on an underlying security is bullish. Learn how to use a Bull Condor Spread.

Bullish: An expectation that an option, or any financial instrument, will increase in price.

Bullish Trading Strategies: Strategies that can be used to profit from an upward move in the price of a financial instrument. List of Bullish Strategies.

Bull Market: When the overall market is moving upwards.

Bull Put Spread: A simple strategy, involving puts, which can be used when the expectation is that the underlying security will increase in price. Learn how to use a Bull Put Spread.

Bull Spread: A spread that is created to profit from bullish movements.

Bull Trap: An unconfirmed market movement which suggests a bull market, but is unconfirmed and ends up with the market moving downward.

Butterfly Spread: This is an advanced strategy that can be used to profit from an underlying security remaining neutral. Learn how to use a Butterfly Spread.

Buy to Close Order: An order that is placed when you want to close an existing short position through buying contracts that you have previously written. Read more about the Buy to Close Order.

Buy To Open Order: An order that is placed when you want to open a new position through buying contracts. Read more about the Buy to Open Order.

C

Calendar Call Spread: This is a simple strategy that can be used to profit from an underlying security remaining neutral. Also known as a Time Call Spread. Learn how to use a Calendar Call Spread.

Calendar Put Spread: This is a simple strategy that can be used to profit from an underlying security remaining neutral.

Also known as a Time Put Spread. Learn how to use a Calendar Put Spread.

Calendar Spread: A type of spread that is created using multiple contracts with different expiration dates. Also referred to as a time spread. Read more about Calendar Spreads.

Calendar Straddle: This is an advanced strategy that can be used to profit from an underlying security remaining neutral. Learn how to use a Calendar Straddle.

Calendar Strangle: This is an advanced strategy that can be used to profit from an underlying security remaining neutral. Learn how to use a Calendar Strangle.

Call: See Call Option. Call is often used instead of the full term.

Called Away: The process that takes place when the writer of calls is required to fulfill their obligation and sell the underlying security at the agreed strike price.

Call Option: A type of option which grants the holder the right, but not the obligation, to buy the relevant underlying security at an agreed strike price. Read more about Calls.

Call Ratio Backspread: An advanced strategy that can be used for profit in a volatile market, when there is a bullish outlook. Learn how to use a Call Ratio Backspread.

Call Ratio Spread: This is an advanced strategy that can be used to profit from an underlying security remaining neutral. Learn how to use a Call Ratio Spread.

Carrying Cost: The implied cost of using capital to purchase financial instruments based on interest incurred from borrowing that capital or interest lost from taking that capital from an interest bearing account.

Cash Settled Option: A type of option in which any profits due to the holder at the point of exercise or expiration are paid in cash rather than an underlying security being transacted. Read more about Cash Settled Options.

Chain: Tables that are used to show various information related to specific options. Read more about Chains.

Chooser Option: A type of option that allows the holder to choose whether it's a call or a put at some point during the term of the contract.

Close: The point at the end of a trading day when the market closes and final prices are calculated.

Closing Order: An order which is used to close an existing position. See Buy To Close Order or Sell To Close Order.

Combination Order: A type of order that combines multiple orders into one.

Commodity Option: A type of option where the underlying security is either a physical commodity or a commodity futures contract.

Compound: A type of option where the underlying security is another contract.

Condor Spread: This is an advanced strategy that can be used to profit from an underlying security remaining neutral. Learn how to use a Condor Spread.

Contingent Order: A type of order that allows for the trader to set specific parameters for exiting a position.

Contract Neutral Hedging: A technique for hedging that involves a trader buying as many options as units of the underlying security they own.

Contract Range: The range between the highest and lowest price that an option contract has been traded at.

Contract Size: The number of units of the underlying security that are covered by a contract. The typical contract size is 100. It should be noted that prices are displayed based on one unit of underlying security. So if an option is listed with an ask price of $2.00, and the contract size is 100, it would cost $200 to buy one contract covering 100 units of the underlying security.

130 | P a g e

Conversion & Reversal Arbitrage: An advanced strategy that involves the use of arbitrage. Read more on conversion & reversal arbitrage at Arbitrage Strategies.

Covered Call: This is a simple strategy that can be used to make a profit from existing stock holdings when they are neutral and they are protected against a short term drop in their price. Learn how to use a Covered Call.

Covered Put: This is an advanced trading strategy that can be used in conjunction with short selling stock to profit if the stock remains neutral; it also protects against a short term rise in their price. Learn how to use a Covered Put.

Credit: Money that is received into a trading account.

Credit Spread: A type of spread that is cash positive – i.e. you receive more for writing the options involved in the spread than you spend on buying the options involved in the spread. Read more about Credit Spreads.

Currency Option: A type of option where the underlying security is a specific currency.

D

Day Order: A type of order that is cancelled at the end of a trading day if it hasn't been filled.

Day Trader: A trader who enters and exits their trading positions within one trading day, often holding onto positions for just a few minutes or hours.

Day Trading: The style of trading used by day traders, where positions are entered and exited within the same trading day. Read more about Day Trading.

Debit: Money that is paid out from a trading account.

Debit Spread: A type of spread that is cash negative i.e. you spend more on buying the options involved in the spread that you receive for writing the options involved in the spread.

Delta Neutral Hedging: A strategy that is used to protect an existing position from small movements in price. This can be used to hedge existing positions in stocks or other financial instruments. Read more about Delta Neutral Hedging.

Delta Neutral Trading: A strategy designed to create trading positions which will neither profit nor loss if there are small movements in the price of the underlying stock, but will return profits if the price of the underlying security moves significantly in either direction. Read more about Delta Neutral Trading.

Delta Value: One of the Greeks, the delta value measures the theoretical effect of changes in the price of the underlying security on the price of the option. Also referred to as Options Delta.

Derivative: A financial instrument which derives its value primarily from the value of another financial instrument. Options are a type of derivative.

Diagonal Spread: A type of spread that is created by using multiple contracts with different expiration dates and different strike prices. Read more about Diagonal Spreads.

Directional Risk: The risk of loss from the price of a security moving in an unfavorable direction. For example, if you write calls you exposed to the directional risk of the underlying security possibly increasing in price.

Directional Outlook: The expectation of which direction, if any, that the price of a security will move in. For example, if you are expecting a security to increase in price you have a bullish outlook.

Discount Broker: A type of broker that carries out transactions at a low price, but generally offers little in the way of additional services. For more information please read Full Service Brokers vs Discount Brokers.

Discount Option: An option that is trading for less than its intrinsic value.

Dividend: A payment that can be made by a company to its shareholders, representing their share of profits.

Dynamic Position: A position which is constantly adjusted as required to serve its purpose.

E

Early Assignment: When the writer of contracts is required to fulfill their obligations under the terms of those contracts before the expiration date; early assignment happens when contracts are exercised early.

Early Exercise: When an American style is exercised before the expiration date.

Employee Stock Options: A type of option that is based on stock in a company and issued to employees of that company: typically as a form of remuneration, bonus, or incentive. Read more about Employee Stock Options.

European Style Option: An options contract that can only be exercised at the point of expiration and not before. Read more about European Style Options.

Exercise: The process by which the holder of a contract uses their right under the terms of that contract to either buy or sell the relevant underlying security at the stated strike price. Learn more about Exercising an Option.

Exercise Limit: A limit on the number that can be exercised that may be imposed on the holder.

Exercise Price: See Strike Price

Expiration Date: The date on which a contract expires and effectively ceases to exist. Options must be exercised on or before this date, or they will expire worthless.

Expire Worthless: When a contract reaches the expiration date and has no value i.e. it's either at the money or out of the money at the point of expiration.

Expiry: See Expiration Date.

Extrinsic Value: The component of a price that is affected by factors other than the price of the underlying security, such as time left until expiration. Read more on the following page: Price of Options.

F

Fiduciary Call: A strategy that is designed to effectively cover the costs of exercising a call. Read more about Fiduciary Calls.

Fill Or Kill Order: Often abbreviated to FOK, this is a type of order that must be either filled with immediate effect or cancelled.

Financial Instrument: A real or virtual asset that has an inherent monetary value and/or transfers monetary value. Stocks, shares, options, currencies, futures, and commodities are all forms of financial instruments.

Fundamental Analysis: A style of analyzing the value of a financial instrument by studying certain specific factors that relate to the true value of that security. Studying the financial reports of a company would be a way to carry out fundamental analysis on stock in that company.

Futures Option: A type of option where the underlying security is a future contract.

Full Service Broker: A type of broker that offers expert advice and professional guidance in addition to executing orders for a client; they typically charges higher fees and commissions.

G

Gamma Neutral Hedging: A hedging technique that involves creating positions where the overall gamma value is as close to zero as possible so that the delta value of the positions should remain static whether or not the price of the underlying security moves up or down.

Gamma Value: One of the Greeks, the gamma value measures the theoretical effect of changes in the price of the underlying security on the delta value of that option.

Going Long: Taking a long position on a financial instrument with the expectation that it will increase in price over time. Buying a contract is going long on that option.

136 | P a g e

Going Short: Taking a short position on a financial instrument with the expectation that it will decrease in price. Writing a contract is going short on that option.

Good Until Cancelled: Often abbreviated to GTC, this is a type of order that stays active until it is either filled or cancelled.

Greeks: A series of values that can be used to measure the sensitivity of an option to changes in market conditions and the theoretical changes in the price of an option caused by specific factors such as the price of the underlying security, volatility, and time left until expiry. Read more about the Greeks.

H

Hedge / Hedging: An investment technique used to reduce the risk of holding a specific investment. Options are commonly used as hedging tools: protecting another's existing position or a position in another financial instrument such as stock.

Historical Volatility: Often abbreviated to HV, a measure of the volatility of the price a financial instrument over a specified period in the past.

Holder: The owner of options contracts.

Horizontal Spread: A type of spread that's created using multiple contracts with different expiration dates, but with the same strike price. Read more about Horizontal Spreads.

I

Immediate Or Cancel Order: Often abbreviated to IOC, this is a type of order that must be partially or filled immediately or cancelled. If the order is only partially completed, the balance of the order is cancelled.

Implied Volatility: Often abbreviated to IV, it's a measure of the estimated volatility of the price a financial instrument at the current time. Read more about Volatility and Implied Volatility.

Index Option: A type of option where the underlying security is an index, such as the S & P 500.

In The Money Option: An option where the price of the underlying security is in a favorable position, relative to the strike price, for the holder: meaning it has intrinsic value. A call is in the money when the price of the underlying security is higher than the strike price and a put is in the money when the price of the underlying security is lower than the strike price.

Intrinsic Value: The component of a price that's affected by the profit that is effectively built into a contract when it's in the money – i.e. the amount of theoretical profit that could be realized by exercising the option.

Iron Albatross Spread: This is an advanced strategy that can be used to profit from an underlying security remaining neutral. Learn how to use an Iron Albatross Spread.

Iron Butterfly Spread: This is an advanced strategy that can be used to profit from an underlying security remaining neutral. Learn how to use an Iron Butterfly Spread.

Iron Condor Spread: This is an advanced strategy that can be used to profit from an underlying security remaining neutral. Learn how to use an Iron Condor Spread.

L

LEAPS: The acronym for Long Term Equity Anticipation Securities. These are contracts that expire several months, or longer, in the future.

Leg: When an options position is made up of a combination of multiple positions, each of the individual positions is known as a leg.

Legging: The process of entering or exiting a position that is made up of a combination of multiple positions by transacting each position individually. Read more about Legging.

Legging In: See Legging; the process of entering a position using legging.

Legging Out: See Legging; the process of exiting a position using legging.

Level II Quotes: Also known as Level 2 Quotes. Real time quotes that are provided by exchanges detailing the exact bid ask

139 | P a g e

spreads being offered by market makers. Typically used by very active traders to get the best possible prices at any given time.

Leverage: The use of specific financial instruments, such as options, to get a greater potential return on invested capital, or the use of borrowed capital to achieve potentially greater profits. Read more about Leverage.

Limit Order: A type of order used to buy or sell financial instruments at a specified maximum or minimum price respectively.

Limit Stop Order: Also known as a stop limit order, an order to close a position when a certain price is reached, if the order can be filled within a specified limit.

Liquidity: A measure of the ease with which a financial instrument can be bought or sold without impacting the price, or the ease with which a financial instrument can be converted to cash.

Listed Option: A type of option that is listed on an exchange, with fixed strike prices and expiration dates.

Long: You are long on a financial instrument if you own that instrument and/or you stand to gain from it increasing in price.

Long Call: This is a simple strategy that can be used when the outlook on an underlying security is bullish. Learn how to use a Long Call.

Long Gut: This is a simple strategy that can be used when price of the underlying security is volatile and expected to move significantly, but the direction of the move is unclear. Learn how to use a Long Gut.

Long Position: The position of being long on a financial instrument. If you own options contracts, then you hold a long position on them.

Long Put: This is a simple strategy that can be used when the outlook on an underlying security is bearish. Learn how to use a Long Put.

Long Straddle: This is a simple strategy that can be used when the price of the underlying security is volatile. Learn how to use a Long Straddle.

Long Strangle: This is a simple strategy that can be used when price of the underlying security is volatile and expected to move significantly, but the direction of the move is unclear. Learn how to use a Long Strangle.

Look Back Option: A type of option that allows the holder to exercise the option at the best price that underlying security reached during the life of the option. Read more about Look Back Options.

M

Margin: Margin has multiple meanings depending on the context that it's being used in. Margin related to buying stocks is the process of borrowing capital from a broker to buy stocks. Margin related to options trading is the amount of cash required to be held in a trading account when writing contracts. Read more about Margin.

Market Makers: Professional, high volume traders that are generally employees of financial institutions and are responsible for ensuring there's adequate depth and liquidity within the market for it to run efficiently. Read more about Market Makers.

Market On Close Order: Often abbreviated to MOC, this is a type of order that is filled at the end of a trading day.

Market Order: A type of order used to buy or sell financial instruments at the current market price. A market order will always be filled providing there's a corresponding seller or buyer.

Market Stop Order: Also known as a stop market order, an order to close a position at market price when a certain price is reached.

142 | P a g e

Married Puts: A hedging strategy that uses stocks and options. Read more about Married Puts.

Moneyness: A method used to measure the relationship of the strike price of an option to the current price of the underlying security. Read more about Moneyness.

Morphing: The changing of one position into another position with just one order, typically used with synthetic positions.

N

Naked Option: Also known as an uncovered option, this is where the writer of a contract doesn'tt have a corresponding position in the underlying security to protect them against unfavorable price movements. For example, writing calls without owning enough of the underlying security is writing naked options or taking a naked position.

Near The Money Option: An option where the price of the underlying security is very close to the strike price.

Neutral Market: When the overall market is relatively stable it's either bullish or bearish.

Neutral Outlook: An expectation that the market, or a specific financial instrument, will remain relatively stable in price.

Neutral Trading Strategies: Strategies that can be used to profit from the price of a financial instrument not moving, or moving only slightly. List of Neutral Strategies.

O

One Sided Market: A market where the buyers outnumber the sellers or the sellers significantly outnumber the buyers.

One Cancel Other Order: Often abbreviated to OCO, this is a type of combination order where one order is cancelled when the other one is filled.

One Trigger Other Order: Often abbreviated to OTO, this is a type of combination order where one order is automatically executed when the other one is filled.

Online Broker: A broker that enables you to enter your orders using an online trading platform.

Opening Order: An order that is used to open a new position. See Buy To Open Order or Sell To Open Order.

Open Interest: A measurement of the total number of open positions relating to a particular option. Read more about Open Interest.

Optionable Stock: Stock that has options based on it.

Option / Options Contract: The right to buy or sell a specified underlying security at a fixed strike price within a specified period.

Option Pain: The theoretical price of an underlying security that will result in the highest number of traders losing the highest amount of money due to options contracts expiring out of the money.

Options Broker: An individual or a company that executes orders to buy and sell options contracts on behalf of clients. List of the Best Brokers.

Options Trader: Any investor that buys and/or sells options contracts.

Options Trading: The process of buying and/or selling options contracts as a form of investment, to make short term profits, or to hedge existing positions.

Options Symbol: Effectively the name of an option; a string of characters that defines specific options contracts.

Out Of The Money Option: An option where the price of the underlying security is in an unfavorable position, relative to the strike price, for the holder: meaning it has no intrinsic value. A call is out of the money when the price of the underlying security is lower than the strike price and a put is out of the money when the price of the underlying security is higher than the strike price.

Outlook: An expectation on which direction, if any, the market or a specific underlying security will move.

Over The Counter Option: A type of option that is only sold over the counter (OTC) and not on the public exchanges. They are typically highly customized options with specific parameters.

P

Physical Option: An option where the underlying security is a physical asset that is neither stock nor futures contracts.

Physically Settled Option: A type of option in which the underlying security changes hands between the holder and the writer of the options when it's exercised.

Portfolio: The combined holdings of any financial instruments owned by an individual, group, or financial institution.

Position Trader: A trader who uses the unique opportunities that options offer to profit from factors such as time decay and volatility.

Position Trading: The style of trading used by position traders, who are usually very experienced traders, to take advantage of the opportunities for profit that are created by the mechanics of options trading. Read more about Position Trading.

Premium: A term that can be used to describe the whole price of an option or the extrinsic value of an option. Read more about Premium.

Pricing Model: A mathematical formula that is used to value or price an option contract based on specific factors. See Black Scholes Pricing Model or Binomial Pricing Model for examples.

Pricer: A specific type of chain that displays the five main Greeks in addition to other standard information.

Protective Call: A strategy that is used to protect profits in a short stock position.

Protective Put: A strategy that is used to protect profits in a long stock position. Learn how to use a Protective Put.

Put: A type of option which grants the holder the right, but not the obligation, to sell the relevant underlying security at an agreed strike price. Read more about Put Options.

Put Call Parity: A concept related to pricing that's based on avoiding arbitrage by ensuring the extrinsic values of related calls and when puts are equal, or close to equal in value.

Put Ratio Backspread: An advanced strategy that can be used for profit in a volatile market, when there's a bearish outlook. Learn how to use a Put Ratio Backspread.

Put Ratio Spread: This is an advanced strategy that can be used to profit from an underlying security remaining neutral. Learn how to use a Put Ratio Spread.

R

Ratio Spread: A type of spread that is created using multiple contracts of differing amounts. This typically involves writing a higher amount of options than is being bought, but the ratio can be either way around. Read more about Ratio Spreads.

Realize A Profit: The process of taking profits when closing an existing a position. Profit that exists in an open position is unrealized profit.

Realize A Loss: The process of incurring losses when closing an existing position. Losses that exist in an open position are unrealized.

Resistance Level: A price point, higher than its current price, that a financial instrument has not risen above over a given period.

Return On Investment: Often abbreviated to ROI, this is the percentage of profit that's made, or could be made, on an investment.

Reverse Iron Albatross Spread: An advanced strategy that can be used to make returns from a volatile market. Learn how to use a Reverse Iron Albatross Spread.

Reverse Iron Butterfly Spread: An advanced strategy that can be used to make returns from a volatile market. Learn how to use a Reverse Iron Butterfly Spread.

Reverse Iron Condor Spread: An advanced strategy that can be used to make returns from a volatile market. Learn how to use a Reverse Iron Condor Spread.

Rho Value: One of the Greeks, the rho value measures the theoretical effect of changes in interest rates on the price of the option. Also referred to as Options Rho.

Risk Graph: A graph used to illustrate the risk to reward ratio of a position. Read more about Risk Graphs.

Risk Reversal: A simple strategy that's typically used for hedging. Read more about Risk Reversal.

Risk To Reward Ratio: An indication of how much risk is involved in a position about the potential rewards or profits. Read more about Risk to Reward Ratio.

ROI: See Return on Investment.

Rolling Down: The process of closing an existing position and opening a comparable position at the same time, but with a lower strike price.

Rolling Forward: The process of closing an existing position and opening a comparable position at the same time, but extending the time left until expiry.

Rolling: A trading technique used to close an existing position and open a similar one at the same time, with slightly different terms. Read more about Rolling.

Rolling Up: The process of closing an existing position and opening a comparable position at the same time, but with a higher strike price.

S

Sell To Close Order: An order that's placed when you want to close an existing long position through selling the contracts you have previously bought.

Sell To Open Order: An order that's placed when you want to open a new position through writing new contracts. Read more about the Sell to Open Order.

Settlement: The process by which the terms of a contract are resolved when the option is exercised.

Short: You are short on a financial instrument if you have short sold that financial instrument and/or you stand to gain from it falling in price.

Short Albatross Spread: An advanced strategy that can be used when the market is volatile.

Short Bear Ratio Spread: This is an advanced strategy that can be used when the outlook on an underlying security is bearish.

Short Bull Ratio Spread: This is an advanced strategy that can be used when the outlook on an underlying security is bullish.

Short Butterfly Spread: An advanced strategy that can be used when the market is volatile.

Short Calendar Straddle: An advanced strategy that can be used to profit from volatile market conditions.

Short Calendar Strangle: An advanced strategy that can be used to profit from volatile market conditions.

Short Call: This is a simple strategy that can be used when the outlook on an underlying security is bearish.

Short Call Calendar Spread: An advanced strategy that can be used to profit from volatile market conditions.

Short Condor Spread: An advanced strategy that can be used when the market is volatile.

Short Gut: This is a simple strategy that can be used to profit from an underlying security remaining neutral.

Short Position: The position of being short on a financial instrument. If you write contracts then you hold a short position on them.

Short Put: This is a simple strategy that can be used when the outlook on an underlying security is bullish. Learn how to use a Short Put.

Short Put Calendar Spread: An advanced strategy that can be used to profit from volatile market conditions.

Short Selling: The selling of a financial instrument that isn't currently owned, with the expectation of buying it back in the future at a lower price.

Short Straddle: This is a simple strategy that can be used to profit from an underlying security remaining neutral. Learn how to use a Short Straddle.

Short Strangle: This is a simple strategy that can be used to profit from an underlying security remaining neutral.

152 | P a g e

Spread: A position that's created by buying and/or selling different contracts on the same underlying security to combine multiple positions into one effective position.

Spread Order: A type of order that's used to create a spread by simultaneously transacting all the required trades.

Stock Option: A type of option where the underlying security is stock in a publically listed company.

Stock Repair Strategy: A strategy that's used to recover losses from held stock that has fallen in value.

Stock Replacement Strategy: A strategy that involves buying deep in the money call options instead of the underlying stock. The strategy is used to reduce the capital required to enter the position.

Stop Limit Order: See Limit Stop Order.

Stop Market Order: See Market Stop Order.

Stop Order: A type of order that's used to automatically close a position when a specified price is reached.

Strap Straddle: This is a simple strategy that can be used when price of the underlying security is volatile, but the inclination occurs when the move will be to the upside.

Strap Strangle: This is a simple strategy that can be used when the price of the underlying security is volatile, but the inclination occurs when the move will be to the upside.

Strike Arbitrage: An advanced strategy that involves the use of arbitrage. Read more about the strike arbitrage at Arbitrage Strategies.

Strike Price: The price specified in a contract at which the holder of the contract can exercise their option. The strike price of a call is the price at which the holder can buy the underlying security and the strike price of a put is the price at which the holder can sell the underlying security.

Strip Straddle: This is a simple strategy that can be used when the price of the underlying security is volatile, but the inclination occurs when the move will be to the downside.

Strip Strangle: This is a simple strategy that can be used when the price of the underlying security is volatile, but the inclination occurs when the move will be to the downside.

Support Level: A price point, lower than its current price, that a financial instrument hasn't fallen below over a given period.

Swing Trader: A trader who looks for relatively short term price swings and aims to profit from those swings by trading accordingly.

Swing Trading: The style of trading used by swing traders, where positions are usually held for a relatively short period to profit from short term price swings.

Synthetic Long Call: A synthetic position which is essentially the same as owning calls. It involves buying puts and buying the related underlying security.

Synthetic Long Put: A synthetic position which is essentially the same as owning puts. It involves buying calls and short selling the related underlying security.

Synthetic Long Stock: A synthetic position which is essentially the same as owning stocks. It involves buying at the money calls and writing at the money puts on the relevant stock.

Synthetic Position: A position that's created using a combination of stocks and options, or a combination of different positions, to emulate another stock position or option position. Read more about Synthetic Positions.

Synthetic Short Call: A synthetic position which is essentially the same as being short on call options. It involves short selling stock and then writing put options based on that stock.

Synthetic Short Put: A synthetic position which is essentially the same as being short on put options. It involves buying a stock and then writing call options based on that stock.

Synthetic Short Straddle: A synthetic strategy that essentially replicates the Short Straddle trading strategy. Read more about the synthetic short straddle at Synthetic Strategies.

Synthetic Short Stock: A synthetic position which is essentially same as being short on stock. It involves the writing of at the money call options and buying at the money put options on the relevant stock.

Synthetic Straddle: A synthetic strategy that essentially replicates the Long Straddle trading strategy. Read more about the synthetic straddle at Synthetic Strategies.

T

Technical Analysis: A style of analysis used to predict the future price movements of a financial instrument by studying historical data relating to the volume and price. This typically involves analyzing charts and graphs to find patterns and trends.

Theoretical Value: The value of a specific option, or position, that is calculated by a pricing model or other mathematical formulas.

Theta Value: One of the Greeks, the theta value measures the theoretical rate of time decay of that option. Also referred to as Options Theta.

Time Decay: The process by which the extrinsic value diminishes as the expiration date of the option gets closer. Read more about Time Decay.

Time Call Spread: See Calendar Call Spread.

Time Put Spread: See Calendar Put Spread.

Time Spread: See Calendar Spread.

Time Value: See Extrinsic Value

Trading Plan: A detailed plan that a trader would prepare to lay out how they'll approach their trading. The plan would usually include defined objectives, details of methods that will be used for budget control, risk management, and which strategies will be used.

Trailing Stop Order: A type of order that includes a stop price which is based on a percentage or absolute change from the previous best price.

Trading Levels: A level that's assigned to account holders at brokers to indicate what level of risk they can be exposed to. They are used to protect traders that have insufficient capital or inadequate experience from entering trades that they shouldn't have. Also known as approval levels.

Trading Style: The method and/or approach that a trader undertakes to follow; there are several specific types of trading styles. Read more about Types of Options Trader & Trading Style.

Trend: A recognizable and continued movement in a market or the price of a specific financial instrument.

V

Vega Value: One of the Greeks, the vega value measures the theoretical effect of changes in the implied volatility of the underlying security on the price of the option. Also referred to as Options Vega.

Vertical Spread: A type of spread that's created using multiple contracts with different strike prices, but it has the same expiration dates. Read more about Vertical Spreads.

Volatile: A financial instrument or whole market, that's moving unexpectedly and/or dramatically is said to be volatile.

Volatile Market: A market that's constantly moving unexpectedly and dramatically, with a high level of price instability.

Volatile Trading Strategies: Strategies that can be used to profit from a volatile market and/or a volatile financial instrument. List Of Volatile Strategies.

Volatility: A measure of how a financial instrument is expected to fluctuate over a specified period. Read more about Volatility.

Volatility Crunch: A significant drop in implied volatility.

Volatility Skew: When a graph that represents the implied volatility across options with the same underlying security, but different strike prices form a curve skewed to right.

Volatility Smile: When a graph that represents the implied volatility across options has the same underlying security but different strike prices, forms a concave similar in appearance to a smile.

Volume: The amount of transactions that took place involving a specified financial instrument such as a particular option. One with a high volume means it has been heavily traded.

W

Weekly Option: A type of option that uses a weekly expiration cycle.

Writer: The creator of new contracts to sell.

Writing An Option: The process of effectively creating new contracts to sell.

Conclusion

Options are a financial product that give you the right to buy or sell an underlying asset at a specific price, on a specific date. They're built around giving you the option to pass if the contract expires in an unprofitable position. If you would make money, you can exercise your contract. If you would lose money, you can simply walk away.

There are options strategies like the above that are simple and can be put to use by beginner investors. There are also incrementally complex options strategies that involve two to four transaction stages. There are also different call and put options, in the money, out of the money and at the money. Each has the potential to give you desired outcome based on your market expectation or when you are unclear about the direction of the markets and want to hedge your price risks on both upside or downside. One of the most significant advantages of options strategies is, they enable you to make profits even when you do not know in which direction the price movements are headed. Then, there are other strategies where you take a well-calculated call on how much the volatility is going to be or whether prices will remain stable. These are essential hedging tools and can be used by investors who are beginners in their journey of stock investing.

Trading is difficult. But it is not a mystical ability and it can be learned. Here we have broken the trading process into the parts that a professional trader needs: an understanding of market structure, an understanding of the instruments he trades, a way to capture edge, and a methodology for managing risk. This is necessary for all traders, not only those who specialize in options. It is also the approach that the large option trading firms have been built upon.

Knowledge of market structure is probably the aspect of this approach that most distinguishes professional traders from amateurs. This is sometimes dismissed as being merely administrative. It certainly is administrative but to be dismissive to this aspect of trading is to invite failure. A solid understanding of infrastructure can directly lead to profits.

For example, negotiating a better funding rate than one's competitors allows a trader to become a lender to other option traders by actively making markets in boxes. Good infrastructure also makes risk control easier. It may seem trivial to have the phone number of one's clearing firm on hand, but knowing this can easily save money in the event of technical problems. If in doubt, it is better to be overcautious when it comes to such mere administration.

The fact that we need knowledge of options to trade them should be obvious. Exactly what knowledge is worth acquiring does not seem to be as apparent. A trader does not need to know how to derive ...

CPSIA information can be obtained
at www.ICGtesting.com
Printed in the USA
LVHW051158220221
679611LV00009B/365